MUSICAL COMEDY

MUSICAL
COMEDY

A Story in Pictures

by

RAYMOND MANDER & JOE MITCHENSON

Foreword by NOËL COWARD

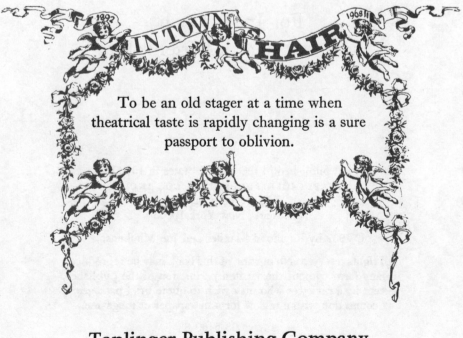

To be an old stager at a time when
theatrical taste is rapidly changing is a sure
passport to oblivion.

Taplinger Publishing Company

New York

'Dedicate your book to me'
SALLY BOWLES—*Cabaret*

For Judi Dench
with our love and friendship

First published in the United States in 1970 by
TAPLINGER PUBLISHING CO., INC.
29 East Tenth Street
New York, New York 10003

© 1969 by Raymond Mander and Joe Mitchenson

SBN 8008-5460-8

Library of Congress Catalog Number 70-94125

PRINTED IN GREAT BRITAIN

CONTENTS

Foreword by Noël Coward

On my fifth birthday my mother injected the 'musical comedy' virus into my bloodstream by taking me to see *The Dairymaids* at the Grand Theatre, Croydon. All I can clearly remember of it is the opening chorus in an elaborate dairy where a number of young ladies were skittishly manipulating butter churns, and the opening chorus of the second act when, confusingly, the same young ladies were vaulting about in a gymnasium in a high school and executing a complicated dance routine with Indian clubs. Delighted but bewildered by all this, I questioned my mother closely, but her explanations were vague and unsatisfying. However, it established in my mind the conviction that 'musical comedy' was gaily irrational to the point of lunacy, a conviction which I have staunchly upheld for over sixty years.

My mother was what would be described in today's American slang as 'a genuine musical comedy buff'. This is easily accounted for by the fact that, during her early married years, she appeared humbly but repeatedly in the chorus of the Teddington Amateur Dramatic Society's productions of Gilbert and Sullivan. When she took me to the theatre for birthday and other treats it was always to a musical comedy, in fact I never saw a 'straight' play until I was eleven and had already been on the stage professionally for a year. This first 'straight' play I saw was a comedy called *Better Not Enquire*, starring Charles Hawtrey, at the Prince of Wales Theatre. No prescient inner voice whispered to me that within six months I should be appearing at that same theatre with Hawtrey himself, in a play called *The Great Name*, in which I had one line, as a page-boy, in the last act.

In those early years my favourite musical-comedy actress was Miss Gracie Leigh, who always played second (soubrette) parts. In the window of Keith Prowse I saw a poster advertising *The Quaker Girl* on which she headed the female cast list. There was another poster overlapping this, and so it was not until Mother and I had forced our way into the front row of the pit and opened our programme that we noticed the four magic words 'And Miss Gertie Millar'. Presently she made her entrance with all the Quakers, detached herself from them, glided across the stage to Joseph Coyne, who was sitting under a tree, and proceeded to sing and dance their first duet, 'When a Good Good Girl like Me meets a Bad Bad Boy like You'. From that moment onwards I was enslaved. Many years later I went, with her, to the opening night of a revival of *The Quaker Girl* which was less than adequately performed and I remember her putting her hand gently on my knee to calm my irritated twitchings and quell my muttered imprecations. To me Gertie Millar was, and is—now, alas, only in my memory—the epitome of what a musical-comedy star should be, as indeed *The Quaker Girl* was the epitome of what a musical comedy should be. It has a good story, excellent lyrics and, above all, an enchanting score by Lionel Monckton. Embedded in my mind for ever is the vision of Gertie Millar singing 'Tony from America' in the moonlit garden of the 'Pre-Catalan', moving with such feather-light grace that she seemed to be floating rather than dancing.

Messrs Mander and Mitchenson, having produced this lucid and comprehensive survey of musical comedy over the years, flatteringly invited me to write a Foreword to it, an invitation which I accepted with alacrity. It wasn't until I had read their manuscript that the full extent of their shameless perfidy dawned upon me. Being tireless and meticulous researchers, they have cunningly blocked the path to any appraisals and facts that I might have written by unequivocally stating them themselves. Unfortunately they have done this so well that I cannot, in all honesty, score my pen through their damned accuracies and appropriate them for myself, so I am left, like poor Manon, in an arid waste, solo, perduto e abandonato. (Her arid waste was, inexplicably, near New Orleans, mine near Montreux.)

In the days of my youth musical-comedy stars were a good deal more insouciant in regard to their work and their public than they are today. They 'stayed off' on the slightest pretext. I remember waiting for hours in pit and gallery queues to see Lily Elsie in *The Merry Widow*, *The Dollar Princess* and *The Count of Luxembourg*, but I never actually caught up with her until she played *Pamela* at the Palace Theatre during the Great War. She was, of course, enchanting; but I cannot resist sending an affectionate 'Thank you' back over the years to Miss Deborah Volar, her understudy, whom I saw so often and knew so much better. I was much luckier with my adored Gertie Millar, on one occasion miraculously so. I opened my programme and there was the sinister little slip announcing that 'Owing to indisposition, etc., Miss Millar's part would be played by Miss Whoever-it-was'. I groaned with disappointment and contemplated for a moment leaving the theatre, but as I was being taken as a special treat by an old friend who had booked the seats (dress circle, front row) weeks before, I crushed down my gloom and determined to enjoy the show for what it was worth. It was fortunate that I did, because on she came, my beloved star, as magical as ever. Of course, the age-old tradition that a star must appear even if he or she is practically dying is an excellent one, although it can be carried too far. I once played a performance of *The Knight of the Burning Pestle* with a temperature of 103 and gave sixteen members of the company mumps, thereby closing the play and throwing everybody out of work. There may be a moral lurking somewhere in this, but I cannot for the life of me discover what it is.

To return to the subject of the Foreword, 'Musical Comedy'. Musical comedy was, I believe, originally devised by the late George Edwardes as a happy compromise between the continental operettas of Lecocq and Offenbach, the early burlesques of the old Gaiety Theatre and the healthy, clean-limbed but melodious high jinks of Gilbert and Sullivan. In my youth nearly all musical comedies had 'Girl' titles: *The Girl from Kay's*, *The Girl from Up There*, *The Girl in the Taxi*, *The Girl on the Film*, *The Sunshine Girl*, *The Girl from Utah*, *The Girl in the Train*, and so on. Every now and then a 'Maid' or two edged their way on to the posters: *The Spring Maid*, *My Mimosa Maid*, *The Maid of the Mountains*. But on the whole the 'Girls' won hands down.

In most of these entertainments there was nearly always a bitter misunderstanding between the hero and the heroine at the end of the first act (if it was in two acts) or the second act (if it was in three acts). Either he would insult her publicly on discovering that she was a princess in her own right rather than the simple commoner he had imagined her to be, or she would wrench his engagement ring from her finger, fling it at his feet and faint dead away on hearing that he was not the humble tutor she had loved for himself alone, but a multi-millionaire. The ultimate reconciliation was usually achieved a few seconds before the final curtain, after the leading comedian had sung a topical song and there was nothing left to do but forgive and forget. The musical comedies of today are less encumbered with social overtones: the problems of disguised princes and princesses have given way to the more realistic machinations of spies and crooks and gangsters, who provide more excitement perhaps but, for me, less nostalgia. I still miss the anguished second-act-finale misunderstanding between the hero and the heroine and I still long to hear the leading lady cry with a breaking heart, 'Play louder—play louder. I want to dance and forget!' Personally I have not the least desire for the music to play louder and I certainly do not want to dance and forget. What I do want, however, and what I fully intend to do is to look back over the years and, with a grateful smile, remember.

The Story of Musical Comedy

Music and dance were combined from the very caverns of time, but to search there for the origins of English musical comedy is to get lost in a welter of words and sounds which mean little, except to the scholarly musicologists.

After the days of the liturgical drama, which was naturally linked with music, came the secular masque. Originally for the most part a court entertainment under the Tudors, it achieved its greatest triumphs in Jacobean times with the work of Ben Jonson and his associated musicians, as a spectacular, dramatic and musical entertainment.

In the later work of Shakespeare masques began to reach the public playhouses. *The Tempest* in 1611 contained a classical masque conjured up by Prospero for the entertainment of the young lovers, Ferdinand and Miranda.

Milton's *Comus*, produced in 1634, and similar now-forgotten works provide the link with the first English opera, *The Siege of Rhodes*, written by Sir William Davenant to music of five composers, produced privately under the Commonwealth in 1656. Strangely enough this form was brought into being in this country as a union of words and music during the closure of the public playhouses and the ban on the spoken drama by the Puritans.

After the Restoration lighter pastorals and ballad operas take the stage of the two theatres operating under Royal Patent, side by side with the serious dramas, the actors and actresses often appearing in both forms. Eventually the rarefied atmosphere of the newly introduced Italian grand opera was to find a home and interpreters in its own opera house in 1705.

Colley Cibber, ever ready to follow if not create fashion, adapted his own comedy *Love in a Riddle* into a pastoral ballad opera, *Damon and Phillida*, in 1729. This followed on the phenomenal success in 1728 of *The Beggar's Opera*, itself called a Newgate Pastoral, and set a fashion for the parody of the loftier realms of opera, which was to last for at least the next 150 years.

The more gentle and romantic ballad operas of Thomas Arne, Thomas Dibdin, William Shield and Henry Bishop span the reigns of the four Georges and cover the transition into the period of the highflown romantic British opera of the early Victorian era, as still remembered in the works of Balfe, Benedict and Vincent Wallace.

The restrictions under which theatrical productions then operated dated back to the Restoration, when two Charters or Patents were granted by Charles II for a King's Company and a Duke of York's Company. This created a monopoly of the spoken or legitimate drama, vested in the two companies; words combined with music and mime (which covered opera and ballet) were unspecified and outside the terms provided. The King's Company became established in its own Theatre Royal, Drury Lane, in 1663, and the second Patent, after many vicissitudes, became vested in the Theatre Royal, Covent Garden, from 1732.

The Little Theatre in the Haymarket, which had opened illegally in defiance of the Patentees, in 1720, achieved a restricted Royal Charter in 1766. The new Haymarket

Opera House, opened in 1705 as the Queen's Theatre (later the King's and Her Majesty's), being an opera house, was outside the conditions of the Patents and was licensed by the Lord Chamberlain. From 1737 all the theatres came under the direct jurisdiction of the Lord Chamberlain when Henry Fielding's continual flouting of authority, with his political satires at the Little Theatre in the Haymarket, caused Sir Robert Walpole to introduce censorship.

The breaking of this jurisdiction was achieved in two stages, first in 1843 when the Licensing Act broke the monopoly of the Theatres Royal and in 1968 when the rule of the Lord Chamberlain ended.

In the early years of the nineteenth century, when to cater for the fast-growing working-class population 'minor' theatres were opening in central London and the outer suburbs, they could only operate on what became known as a Burletta Licence. This way round the law allowed, under a magistrate's licence, music and dancing and only those plays which included five musical items in each act or a musical accompaniment. Melo-Drama which came into being in this country in 1802 was ideal for this purpose. The production of legitimate drama, both classical and contemporary, was forbidden, but ways round the situation were found. For instance, songs, or a chord struck on a piano-forte in the orchestra pit at intervals during the performance of a drama, was held by some to be within the limits of the licence: but any management contravening the law was open to prosecution on information laid before the magistrates by a Common Informer, usually at the instigation of one of the Patent theatres, if a minor theatre manager was too bold or flagrant in his defiance of the situation.

Small theatres were opened from time to time and Assembly Halls were adapted for theatrical use, calling themselves Subscription Theatres. This meant no money was taken at the doors, and many were the subterfuges designed to sell tickets—the purchase of sweets or a cup of coffee in adjoining premises allowing free admission to the place of entertainment was a favourite device. But at best many of the lesser managers led a precarious existence at the mercy of the law.

Plays old and new treated as 'musical pieces' led to the fully integrated and more sophisticated burlettas, extravaganzas and burlesques of Planché and his followers, and became the roots of the family tree of twentieth-century revue.

The breaking of the monopoly in 1843 left the field clear for the total division of the West End theatres and the artists themselves into 'legitimate' and 'musical'. By 1850 Music Hall had come into being in premises operated under a licence for singing and dancing only, the continuous spoken word, as dialogue, being forbidden. This, together with lurid melodramas, which had now become the stock in trade of the minor theatres, provided the entertainment of the working-class masses.

Burlesques of classical, historical, literary or operatic subjects written by the Broughs and H. J. Byron and other similar writers together with the early work of W. S. Gilbert provided the staple fare of the Victorian West End musical stage, and were soon joined by operettas and comic operas from France, Germany and Austria, all adapted and well Anglicized!

The writers of burlesque took well-known stories, gave them a modern or topical twist, larded the dialogue with puns and verbal wit and spiced it with songs adapted to familiar music gathered from opera, ballads and the music halls.

Burlesque was always played in 'fantastic' costume, a strange mixture of period, modern and pure invention. Today we would call it 'pantomime' costume. While burlesque drew its themes from a wide range of subjects, operetta and comic opera took their plots from historical, classical or romantic literature and were costumed accordingly. Very seldom did a contemporary plot or dress appear; Strauss's *Die Fledermaus*, at the Alhambra in 1876, is a rare exception. Comic opera, with large injections of ballet, sometimes displayed excessively the female form divine, and even drew at times on the halls for its performers.

The theatres which specialized in these entertainments, the Gaiety, the Alhambra, the Folly and the Royal Strand, were looked on by the vast respectable Victorian middle class as far too Bohemian for their tastes, and the well-proportioned leading ladies and chorus were regarded as being distinctly fast. It was this audience, alien to both music hall and continental operetta, that Gilbert and Sullivan in the eighties, under the far-seeing managerial eye of D'Oyly Carte, sought to attract to the theatre with their polite respectable comic operas.

Ballet dancing as such was frowned upon and discreet, simple dancing, never going even as far as a skirt dance, was *de rigeur*! The Savoy did much to break the continental spell and remove the 'naughty' flavour which hung over the musical stage.

Burlesque with its own Bohemian audiences retreated gradually from the Royal Strand to its last stronghold, the Gaiety, where John Hollingshead had lit what he called 'The Sacred Lamp of Burlesque' in 1868. When he retired in 1886 and handed over to George Edwardes the lamp had lost a little of its lustre and was flickering.

Victorian prejudice was strong, but at times Victorian curiosity was stronger and wily managers found means to satisfy this by subtle subterfuges. From 1880 Augustus Harris even brought those 'dreadfully common music-hall artists' to the sacred precincts of Drury Lane for the annual pantomime, so that they could become respectable at Christmas-time! Even in burlesque injections of new life via music-hall songs (Gaiety versions) were tried. Edwardes actually introduced Lottie Collins herself to sing 'Ta-Ra-Ra-Boom-De-Ay!' in *Cinder-Ellen Up Too Late* in 1891.

Times were changing and managers were searching for new audiences and those audiences could only be won by something itself new, or what appeared to be so. History tells us, if we look hard enough, that nothing ever really happens for the *first* time in one stride without some preparations which are later politely forgotten, if ever consciously noted.

The immediate parents of musical comedy are found not far from the Gaiety at the Royal Strand Theatre, which stood near Somerset House, where Aldwych Tube Station now has its entrance. Here in 1884 the American actress, Minnie Palmer, introduced to the West End a two-year-old 'musical comedy drama' (adapted for English audiences) called *My Sweetheart*, and it had a great success. In 1887 Fannie Leslie, an English actress from burlesque and the halls, played in another 'musical comedy drama' by George R. Sims and Clement Scott called *Jack in the Box*, and in 1891 Charles Arnold, also an American, who had been the original leading man in *My Sweetheart*, put on another adapted importation, *Hans the Boatman*, with a score of 'Home Ballads, Songs and Dances', the work of many hands on both sides of the Atlantic.

In all these shows the characters were ordinary town or country folk wearing contemporary clothes; the world of high society and fashion had yet to invade the 'musical comedy drama'.

It now only needed an imaginative and knowledgeable man of the theatre, understanding the public need of the moment, to weave all those threads, spun in the last decade, into a new backcloth before which to display the exciting new style he could then be said to have 'invented'.

John Hollingshead, at the height of the burlesque era at the Gaiety, was proud to call himself 'A licensed dealer in legs, short skirts, French adaptions, Shakespeare, taste and the musical glasses'. His successor George Edwardes set out, as has every manager since, to follow this example with something new for the jaded palate of the tired businessman. The ingredients were to hand, they only awaited the discovery of the formula.

Later, in 1903, Hollingshead was to write: 'The invention or discovery of Musical Comedy was a happy inspiration of Mr. George Edwardes's. It provided a new form of entertainment for playgoers who go to a theatre for amusement and recreation, which was more elastic in plot or story than the old burlesque. These were generally tied to some well-known tale or legend. This new turn of the dramatic kaleidoscope exhibited a little of the old burletta and the old vaudeville, most of the best elements of farce, a dash of the French *revue*—a stage compound that has never been very fashionable in this country— and much that would not have been out of place in Parisian opera-bouffe. The frame-work would allow of anything being taken out or anything put in, differing in this very little from the Gaiety burlesque, and the term "variety show", applied to many of these productions, had obviously been "lifted" from their predecessors.'

The greatest reaction was in costume. Tights for the ladies and eccentric clothes for the men gave way to exquisite *couture* frocks and Savile Row suits.

One of the biggest factors in forcing a change on the Gaiety was the death in 1892 of Fred Leslie and the protracted illness of Nellie Farren; both were the principal exponents and attraction of burlesque. Edwardes was busy looking around for new artists. Ada Reeve, then a young star on the halls, was approached, but refused to follow in the footsteps of the great Nellie Farren; sensing the changing atmosphere, she preferred to wait her time till the manager could offer her something in a newer mould.

Edwardes now decided to make his experiments away from the Gaiety at his other theatre, the Prince of Wales. He pinned his faith on Arthur Roberts, a great comedian of invention, experienced in burlesque, comic opera and music hall. His authors, Adrian Ross and James Leader, concocted a loosely knit plot which served to introduce songs by Osmond Carr, a composer of merit in the field of light opera. They called their creation *In Town*.

'Captain Coddington, the man about town,' so says a contemporary, 'finds himself in the unpleasant predicament of having invited all the young ladies of the Ambiguity Theatre to luncheon, and being without the wherewithal to pay for their entertainment. To his rescue comes young Lord Clanside, who offers to pay on condition that he shall attend the festivities. Various motives—love, jealousy, interest, etc.—bring his father and mother, the Duke and Duchess, and most of the other characters upon the scene, and in the second act all are transported to the green-room of the Ambiguity during rehearsal. All ends well by the Captain marrying the *prima donna*, and finally overcoming his state of impecuniosity by aid of his ducal patron.'

Gone were the puns and couplets and the familiar plots, though many of the old ingredients, the skirt dance, the interpolated number and the elastic format still remained.

When it opened on 15 October 1892, the Press was quick to see that *In Town*, calling itself 'a musical farce', was something new. The *Sunday Times* said:

'It is difficult to imagine what *In Town* would have been like without Mr. Arthur Roberts. It is a curious medley of song, dance, and nonsense, with occasional didactic glimmers, sentimental intrusions, and the very vaguest attempts at satirising the modern "masher". The main thing is that opportunities are offered for Miss Florence St. John to display her vocal skill and charm in several pretty ballads, from the graceful pen of Mr. Osmond Carr, who, by the way, has written just the kind of tunefully sprightly music suitable to the piece, while Miss Sylvia Grey is enabled to tantalise us with one or two slight dances when we would fain have more, and Mr. Eric Lewis, always a quaint comedian, has some capital songs to sing, and right well he sings them. As for Mr. Roberts, he is a host in himself, and he keeps the whole house in a roar.'

While the *Sunday Sun* reported:

'The result of the experiment is success—success with a very big S. Of all the light and musical entertainments in town just now, and there are many, Mr. Edwardes may congratulate himself that he produced last night the brightest, raciest, and spiciest. Miss Phyllis Broughton is the most irresistibly nice boy that ever trod the boards. Mr. Carr's music is bright and tuneful, and fits the words jauntily. Mr. Roberts is only asked to be himself, which he is to the fullest measure, his movements seeming like a pantomime of epigrams. Miss Florence St. John sings and acts delightfully. Mr. Eric Lewis's *Duke* belongs to a high order of comedy. Miss Sylvia Grey's dances, though they come a little too late, are as airily exquisite as ever; and only space prevents our mentioning other clever minor parts than those of Miss Jennie Roger's call-boy and Mr. Fritz Rimma's hotel porter. The burlesque is really magnificently mounted.'

Another contemporary, *The Players*, is a little more gossipy and fashion conscious:

'Of the story or plot of *In Town* at the Prince of Wales, "God bless you, there's none to tell, Sir!" but as a cheery, bright entertainment, with Mr. Arthur Roberts and a galaxy of female beauty and talent at the helm, it is, or ought to be, quite sufficient for any pleasure-seeker from east to west of our little village. Some very, very smart frocks are worn by the "chorus ladies of the Ambiguity Theatre" in the first act, Miss Maud Hobson being well to the fore in the way of style and presence. Her dress in the first act is quite of the smartest I have seen for some time. The skirt, which is made in a demi-train, lined underneath (and only seen when the wearer moved) with pale pink silk, was composed of a beautiful shade of dove-coloured silk; over this was worn a bodice of the richest purple velvet, designed in a new and very quaint manner, the fronts being cut very long so as to form kind of tabs, stopping short at the side seams and opening over a large Empire sash of black satin, which is taken round high up in front and out again at the back, and fastened there with a large rosette and ends. Miss Hobson wears with this dress a large spoon-shaped bonnet with a black velvet bow, with a diamond brooch underneath the brim in front resting on the hair. At the back, curling over on to the brim in front, is a tuft of black ostrich plumes. The eyes of many of the female portion of the audiences grew large with envy as they watched this creation and its tall and graceful wearer move about the stage. Miss St. John also wore a very pretty visiting gown of bright green silk with some gold embroidery on the skirt and bodice, the latter being made in a very becoming manner on one side. Miss Sylvia Grey had a very smart grey redingote opening over a skirt of the palest rose-pink, pink straw hat, grey feathers, grey gloves and shoes.

'There was a very smart audience, one lady wearing a most beautiful mantle, which took my fancy tremendously. It was made of *turquoise poult-de-soie*, and lined all through with the same material in a most delicate peach colour. The cape—or rather capes, as there were three—were made of a rich deep moss-green velvet with little pleatings all the way round of the turquoise; it was altogether a most dainty confection.'

Later when established as a success and sent on tour it could be said:

'While *In Town* is a reflex of London life and doings, it also illustrates the spirit that actuates English society all over the country, and embodies the very essence of the times in which we live. The characters are types of the day. His Grace the Duke of Duffshire is like a portrait by Frank Holl; du Maurier, in *Punch*, has repeatedly sketched the Duchess, Lady Gwendoline and Lord Clanside; the names of Kitty Hetherton and Flo Fanshawe are looked for among the guests at every smart assembly, and their photographs are in the shop windows; Shrimp, the call-boy, is an *actualité* of an age when the stage and society are closely allied; and even the hall porter of the Hotel Caravanserai is a personality familiar to a world that dines and sups in public. The most prominent stage portrait of all is that of the well-dressed, volatile, ready-witted, but impecunious man about town, who, under the name of Captain Coddington, stands out as a character of the present day, just as Lord Dundreary was typical of his generation. His dress has influenced the fashion of the moment, and his witticisms have become proverbial.'

The impact of the modern fashions seen on the stage was immediately noticeable in the world of the male. The music-hall Lion-comique in the sixties and his successor, including the male impersonator, had dressed themselves in the up-to-the-minute fashion (even if slightly caricatured) as worn by their betters, the smart men about town; they did not create or even lead. Now suddenly the clothes worn by Arthur Roberts and later his successors (George Grossmith and Seymour Hicks) were to set the fashion for the masher, the johnny, or whatever name he was known by at any given moment. Even the London cab driver strove to copy Roberts's clothes in *Gentleman Joe* (*The Hansom Cabby*). Gradually a similar reaction took place in *haute couture*; as women came out of their Victorian cocoon so the musical comedy fashions had their repercussions in everyday life. The ladies of 1907 all wanted to wear a Merry Widow hat. Later Carnaby Street was to rule and the entertainer followed.

After the reception of *In Town* it was obvious to Edwardes and his associates that they were on the right lines. In due course he transferred the production to the Gaiety and produced a second edition with Roberts singing a Gaiety version of "Daddy wouldn't buy me a Bow Wow'. It ran in all 292 performances (it was later revived at the Lyric Theatre in 1897).

Meantime another experiment was made at the Shaftesbury Theatre when on 13 April 1893 a management under the name of F. J. Harris presented *Morocco Bound*, described as 'a musical farcical comedy', by Arthur Branscombe and Adrian Ross with music by Osmond Carr. The cast was headed by Letty Lind, a skirt dancer and *soubrette* and a stalwart of Gaiety burlesque; it also included other artists from Edwardes's management and ran 295 performances. Though Edwardes's name is not mentioned publicly, his participation must be suspected in both this production and its successor, *Go-Bang*.

Strangely Edwardes was still not quite sure of his Gaiety public and tried a revival of a comic opera, *La Mascotte*, by Audran and a new burlesque, *Don Juan*, which opened successfully in October 1893. He had followed his musical-comedy hunch at the Prince of Wales two weeks earlier, on 14 October, with *A Gaiety Girl*, called for the first time 'a Musical Comedy'. This was evolved by a team which for some time was to dominate the musical-comedy world: book by Owen Hall, lyrics by Harry Greenbank and music by Sidney Jones.

'Owen Hall' was a *nom de théâtre*, which both hid and revealed the personality of James Davis, one of a clever Jewish family. His sister, Julia, was 'Frank Danby', the mother of Gilbert Frankau, the novelist, and grandmother of Pamela Frankau. Another sister was Eliza Aria, the 'Mrs. A.' of *Truth*. James Davis was a solicitor with a flair for dramatic and other criticism in which he indulged in his spare time. He had no practical knowledge of the drama, but, in a chance meeting with George Edwardes on a train journey, he told the manager that if he couldn't write a better show than *In Town* he would be damned! Edwardes immediately told him to 'get on with the job' and in a short time the book of *A Gaiety Girl* was born.

The contribution of Owen Hall to the new style of musical comedy was considerable, but an even more important asset was the music of Sidney Jones. This young composer had already written 'Linger Longer, Loo' as a test piece for George Edwardes, who was so impressed by the song that he put it into *Don Juan* with great success, and commissioned him to write the music for the proposed musical comedy. Harry Greenbank, a writer of singable lyrics, was to die young in 1899, but Percy his brother and successor lived till 1968.

Familiar names began to make their appearance on the *A Gaiety Girl* programme, among them Hayden Coffin, Kate Cutler and Marie Studholme. His 'girls', too, had arrived—those statuesque young ladies who moved and wore clothes magnificently, and who were destined, many of them, to make aristocratic marriages and to go down in history as Gaiety Girls.

Though Edwardes was always to put the best of his goods at the front of the stage, the musical side at his theatres was never neglected. The Gaiety had maintained a good regiment of vocal choristers from its earliest days. Often recruited from church choirs, these singers were kept in the background as a reinforcement frequently masked by the scenery or fronted by 'mettle more attractive'.

Of the new piece *The Era* the following Saturday reported:

'Plot is not the "strong point" of the libretto of *A Gaiety Girl*, which was produced, with every sympton of success, at the Prince of Wales Theatre on Saturday last. Mr. Owen Hall has relied—and, as the event proves, not imprudently—upon the witty lines in his dialogue, and upon the attractive qualities of Mr. Harry Greenbank's lyrics and Mr. Sidney Jones's music, to atone for any want of interest in his slight story. The scene of the first act is laid near Windsor Castle. At a garden party given by some officers of the Life Guards, Lady Virginia Forrest is found chaperoning three fashionable young ladies, beguiling the tedium of her task by flirting with Sir Alfred Grey and the Rev. Montague Brierly, the hon. chaplain of the regiment. Major Barclay, an absurd individual, joins the party with some ladies from the Gaiety Theatre, who excite the admiration of the Chaplain, a smug impostor of a familiar type, though they receive the "cold shoulder" from the well-born damsels. Lady Virginia prevails upon the "Gaiety Girls" to give a variety entertainment, which is greatly enjoyed. Alma Somerset, one of the actresses, has honourable proposals made to her by Captain Charles Goldfield, but she refuses to marry him on the ground that she would only injure his position and prospects. A diamond comb is slipped into Alma's pocket by Mina, Lady Virginia's French maid, and Alma is accused of the theft, Captain Goldfield alone believing in her innocence. The second act takes place on the Riviera, where Lady Virginia, the Chaplain and his daughter Rose are staying. It is Carnival time, and Major Barclay masquerades as a brigand, the Judge as a troubadour, and the Chaplain as a Pierrot. In the end Alma's innocence of the theft of which she was accused is demonstrated, it being proved that the comb was placed in her pocket maliciously for the purpose of making her appear a thief.

'This slight outline Mr. Owen Hall and his co-labourers have emboidered and embellished with striking skill. *A Gaiety Girl* is one of the most curious examples of composite dramatic architecture that we have for some time seen. It is sometimes sentimental drama, sometimes comedy, sometimes almost light opera, and sometimes downright "variety show"; but it is always light, bright, and enjoyable. The contrast between certain arts of the piece and other portions is almost startling. From the silly folly of "Jimmy on a Chute" we pass to scenes in which the dialogue is brilliant enough and satirical enough for a comedy of modern life. Line after line goes home to its mark; and the audience are as ready to appreciate the cleverness as they are to enjoy the frivolity of the entertainment. And Mr. Harry Greenbank, the author of the lyrics, has joined in spirit with Mr. Hall in his sharp cuts into the core of modern life.'

Edwardes now knew he had struck a financial gold mine. As the Gaiety was occupied he moved the piece to his other theatre, Daly's, in September 1894 in a revised edition, which ran until December (it was revived in 1899).

On the strength of the success of the earlier *Morocco Bound* 'The New Morocco Bound Company Ltd', a title which must have covered several familiar names, produced another 'musical farcical comedy' called *Go-Bang* at the Trafalgar Square Theatre (the Duke of York's) on 10 March 1894. Again by Adrian Ross and Osmond Carr and directed by Frank Parker, it starred Letty Lind and several Gaiety favourites, besides bringing George Grossmith (the son of the creator of so many Gilbert and Sullivan characters), into the fold. It ran for 159 performances.

The presence of several examples of the 'new' entertainment in the Theatre List and the emergence of other managers in the field began to prove that it was establishing itself in public favour. A revival at the Gaiety of an old burlesque, *Little Jack Sheppard*, in August 1894, caused such a gust of failure that it finally blew out the light of the sacred lamp. The only reward was that it brought to the Gaiety a new up-and-coming young light comedian, Seymour Hicks, and his equally young wife, Ellaline Terriss, full of dainty charm. Edwardes now determined to go the whole way at his principal theatre, and the first Gaiety musical comedy, *The Shop Girl*, was produced on 24 November 1894. The illness of Ellaline Terriss gave Edwardes his opportunity to offer something new, the title role of Bessie Brent, to Ada Reeve, who had been on tour for him in *Don Juan*. Unfortunately previous pantomime commitments only allowed her to stay with the production for a short while and she was followed by several of Edwardes's young ladies before Ellaline Terriss, fully recovered, joined the cast.

Edwardes brought back into his company Letty Lind and others who had been 'away' and recruited George Grossmith, then Jr., to the Gaiety company; he was to remain at the theatre on and off for the next twenty-seven years and spent his life dedicated to the cause of musical comedy both in acting and writing.

The Theatre, a monthly magazine, as always casts a condescending eye over the new production in the January issue:

'If an author is to be judged less by what he does than by his success in accomplishing what he aims at, then Mr. H. J. W. Dam is entitled to distinct praise for his new musical farce *The Shop Girl*. In writing the piece, his principal object has clearly been to cater for the tastes of a Gaiety audience, and there need be no hesitation in admitting that this object he has accomplished very successfully. Inasmuch as his efforts have been sedulously assisted by machinist, costumier, ballet-master, and an exceedingly astute manager, it needs no ghost to come from the grave to predict that a long and prosperous career is in store for the piece.

'On the other hand, there can be detected here and there a certain disposition on the author's part to set at defiance the imperfectly formulated but rapidly crystallizing canons of musical comedy; and to show that the instincts of the playwright are stronger within him than the inclinations of the mere "variety" monger. Luckily, however, for the prosperity of the comedy, such tendencies are born only to be repressed an instant later. In the matter of dialogue, Mr. Dam, if he does not precisely shine, may be said at least to radiate with the brilliancy of a serviceable veneer. His wit lies on the surface, and is, therefore, of a quality to please those who possess neither the desire nor the ability to probe too deeply the mysteries of genuine humour. As the book of the opera is still unpublished, we are unable to speak definitely regarding the merits of the lyrics; but these, at any rate, appear to have been fluently written, and are eminently "settable" to music. Let it also be counted to the author for righteousness that he has provided a more than usually coherent story, which, if a trifle long in starting, progresses merrily enough when once fairly under weigh. Briefly summarized, it deals with the search instituted by a genial millionaire for his old chum's daughter, who, by her father's death, has inherited a tidy fortune of four millions sterling; with the misadventures of a certain Mr. Hooley, proprietor of the Royal Stores, where the missing girl is supposed to be employed, and with the final discovery of the unsuspecting heiress, who meanwhile has pledged her hand to an impecunious youth, who has for long been the happy possessor of her heart.

'It must fairly be said that *The Shop Girl*, as befits her station, is daintily and most sumptuously dressed. Indeed, so splendidly is the little lady apparelled that occasionally one is tempted to forget she is anything more than a lay-figure, intended for the exhibition of magnificent costumes. In this respect, however, she merely fulfils the law of her being. Of the two acts comprised in the piece, the first is decidedly dull, and over-burdened with unnecessary detail; while the second is throughout conspicuously bright and gay. The action of the latter takes place at a fancy bazaar in Kensington, and if Charity, here as elsewhere, serves to cover a multitude of sins, it must be confessed that the sins are of the comeliest and most bewitching description.

'Worthy of special mention are a Japanese dance by Mr. Edmund Payne and Miss Katie Seymour, so quaint, so neat, and so entrancing that it could scarcely fail to subdue the heart of the fiercest Celestial; an extremely graceful *pas seul* by Miss Topsy Sinden; a fascinating dance by Pierrots and Pierrettes, and some very clever travesties by Mr. Edmund Payne, whose entire performance, indeed, deserves the highest praise. In the character of Mr. Hooley, Mr. Arthur Williams was as amusing as the author permitted him to be; but the part lacks humour, and is weighted, moreover, by certain allusions of so questionable a nature as to evoke a very decided protest even from a Gaiety audience. As the heroine, Miss Ada Reeve, although bringing with her something of the atmosphere of the music hall, sang and acted with real brightness and effect, while Mr. Seymour Hicks proved conclusively that a comedian can be funny without vulgarity. A word of commendation is also due to Mr. George Grossmith, jun., who, however, appears to have pretty nearly exhausted all the possibilities of the masher *genus*; Mr. Colin Coop, an excellent singer; Miss Lillie Belmore, a genuine low comedian in petticoats, and to Miss Helen Lee, who at the shortest notice appeared—and with emphatic success—in place of Miss Maud Sherman. Mr. Ivan Caryll has supplied some exceedingly pretty and graceful music, although in point of popularity it may be questioned whether Mr. Lionel Monckton's contributions do not carry off the palm.'

We are taken 'Behind the Scenes' in *The Sketch* on 22 April 1896:

'The stage of the Gaiety Theatre is to the very modern *genus* "Johnny" at once a Mecca and a feast of Tantalus. This is wicked "derangement of epitaphs", as Mrs. Malaprop would have said, but it can be justified. The Gaiety stage is the masher's Mecca; his eyes are continually turned towards it, and yet he is always kept from the

[17]

idols of his heart by a few yards of intervening space. Herein lies the suggestion of Tantalus, which I forbear from amplifying. Nightly the worshippers beset the shrine of the Sacred Lamp, and on the stage the maidens whisper that What's-his-name is in front again this evening. So things have been, so will they be till all burlesques end. And such is fame—to the *genus* "Johnny".

'To the initiated, reverence and enthusiasm are alike denied. When we went to the Gaiety—armed, by courtesy of George Edwardes, with a sop for the actor-managerial, box-official, and stage-managerial heads of Cerberus—our path was free. We followed Mr. Marshall to the side of the stalls, past dense crowds of the young and gilded; an unexpected door yielded to the persuasions of a funny key, and we were on the stage in less time than Oberon's leviathan would have taken to swim across the Strand. For a moment, as though to contradict an eminent phrenologist who declares that I have a hollow in my head where the bump of veneration should be, I stood still and allowed a host of memories to blot out all recognition of the performance in progress, in spite of the fact that our presence was evidently causing some surprise and more amusement.

'Where I stood, Kate Vaughan had rested on the nights when the light of her fame was at its best and brightest; here Letty Lind had passed, fresh from the provinces, with all her world to conquer; Connie Gilchrist had brought London to her feet, and Sylvia Grey had danced our hearts away. Here, too, Florence St. John, Marion Hood, Grace Pedley, and others, had sung the pretty songs written by Meyer Lutz in the days of his consulship; here Nellie Farren had listened to her "boys" as they woke every echo in the house, Arthur Roberts, E. J. Lonnen—just returned from South Africa—poor Fred Leslie, and George Stone—all had paused in their exits where I stood, and had been compelled to return to sing or dance again. Visions of *Frankenstein*, *Little Jack Sheppard*, *Monte Cristo Junior*, *Faust up to Date*, *Ruy Blas*, and *Carmen* came in battalions, and would, perhaps, have stopped, had I not been too busy to entertain them. After all, things had not altered much. Just across the lights, past the orchestra and Ivan Caryll, who was directing it, the men sat as they have been sitting for so many years, immaculate and expressionless. There was a solemnity of shirt-front and eye-glass quite overwhelming, while the occupants of the boxes in the light reflected upon them might have inspired Jan van Beers. It was pleasure that brought Johnny to the Gaiety stalls, but he felt he was performing a solemn duty as well.

'The first sensation connection with the performance was one of surprise at the costume. Nineteenth-century dress had succeeded for once the absence of dress peculiar to the century of Gaiety burlesques. On the prompt side, the "stage beauties" were collecting for their entry in such costume as they might wear in the street. What would an old-time Gaiety girl think of such a condition of things, I wonder? In days of old, the management did not inflict such a strain upon the imagination of its patrons. Perhaps, in *le temps jadis* the "boys" were less cultivated.

'The first act of *The Shop Girl* yields little or nothing descriptive to the watchers in the wings.

'With the termination of the first act, the old Gaiety traditions asserted themselves, and I began to realise that our evening would not be spent in vain. This was evident from the moment when Mr. Hooley's stores were rifled by the army of stage-hands, which moved rapidly to and fro, taking all the paraphernalia to pieces. As shelves and counters receded into dim corners, the cloths of the Japanese bazaar scene came flapping down from above like some wide-winged bird, while portions of kiosks and pavilions followed suit, and high up in the flies, the workmen could be seen hard at their labour.

Soon shapely women, in the traditional Gaiety attire, which was probably originated for summer wear only, came from their dressing-rooms, and either armed themselves with their respective "props", or sat down in the little green-room and looked at a copy of *The Sketch* on the table, or crowded round Mr. Fielders, the patient and clever stage-manager, whose kindness and courtesy were extended to me some years ago when I was on the journalistic threshold. With the change of dress came a change of lighting, giving the stage the old, familiar appearance; and when the curtain rose on the second act, it might have been an old-time burlesque instead of a musical comedy that was in progress. There was a combined sparkle of eyes and diamonds, a *frou-frou* of scant but delicate drapery, as someone came off singing or went on smiling. Presently there came a bevy of fair women and brave men to the "prompt" side, to sing the chorus of the leading lady's song in the wings. A red-coated chorus-master climbed on a chair and directed proceedings. The effect in the dim light was charming, and the voices were well trained and duly sympathetic. From the artistic point of view, it was, perhaps, the best group of the evening, although those in the auditorium saw nothing of it.

'From the front, several of the dresses, or suggestions of dresses, looked somewhat daring, but on the stage they appeared quiet enough. There was such a thoroughly business-like air about proceedings, time and space were so admirably managed and meted out, that a Sunday School meeting, or a prize-distribution at a girls' school, could not have been more free from offence. And as the evening grew late, and the performers warmed to their work, they seemed to be absolutely in sympathy with the audience. Almost since the reign of John Hollingshead the demand has been for up-to-date brightness, for catchy music, topical songs, and pretty faces. Only the low-comedy parts have disappeared, or rather, changed, and the humour of quick change, inebriety, red nose, and impossible trousers has gone to its well-earned rest. He would be a bold man who would disturb its repose.

'But there was nothing further on the stage to yield "copy". The performance itself was for the front of the house to see: there were no startling exits or entrances; the tiny green-room was too crowded to be comfortable. So, with a sigh for the days when such feats were easy of accomplishment, I climbed an almost perpendicular ladder, and, after an apparently endless journey, arrived among the "flies". There the real prose of Stage-land was to be seen. Down below, although everybody was busy, there was no sense of physical labour; but here the men might, in their busiest moments, have been serving Her Majesty against their private inclinations.

'In a world of cords, levers, and pulleys, men directed the setting of the scenes and the raising or lowering of curtains. To their efforts stage lightning and thunder would respond when necessary, and the huge machinery of the stage was practically ruled by their muscles. Below us sections of stage and auditorium were alike distinct, and secrets of head-lights, foot-lights and limelights stood revealed. There was no glamour about such a scene. Mr. Gradgrind himself could not have asked for a more absolute fact. The patient men bending over their limelight, the stage-manager in mufti, and stage-hands standing ready in their corners—all these things contrasted with the glitter and brightness of the stage. And in the auditorium but one side of the picture was seen, and the whole audience was rocking with laughter over the final discomfiture of Mr. Hooley and the strange manners of his shop-girl bride.

'I was still up in the direction of heaven when all the company came upon the stage for the finale. There were all the vivid contrasts of shape, size, colour, and costume, intensified by the seeming confusion, and an increase of enthusiasm due to the proximity of the curtain. At a given signal down it came, and then strong arms drew it skywards for one more brief moment, as though to give the eyes above the sea of shirt-front one last and fond look. Then, as it came down again, the stage was deserted by all its attractions, and only the workmen were left to reduce the once fair bazaars to ruins. By the time I reached the stage the auditorium was empty, the T-pieces were alight, and the holland coverings were being placed over the cushioned seats.'

In all *The Shop Girl* ran for 546 performances and proved that musical comedy was the popular entertainment of the future and had come to stay at the Gaiety.

THE MUSICAL PLAY AT DALY'S

With *The Shop Girl* safely launched at the Gaiety, Edwardes turned his attention to another theatre which needed his guidance. He had originally built Daly's Theatre in 1893 for the American impresario. Augustin Daly, who took the lease, but London did not respond as wholeheartedly to the Americanized classics as he had hoped, and he eventually handed over the lease completely to Edwardes in 1898.

Edwardes had himself used the theatre for a transfer of *A Gaiety Girl* in 1894 and decided to try to create a special brand of musical comedy individually for this theatre. His authors Owen Hall and Harry Greenbank, with Sidney Jones's music, evolved what they now called ' a comedy with music', entitled *An Artist's Model*. It was produced on 2 February 1895, but this first trial was not an initial success. A still rather patronizing critic in *The Theatre* summed up the experiment.

'It is understood that in writing *An Artist's Model*, Mr. Owen Hall, who had already achieved a popular success with *A Gaiety Girl*, set himself the task of raising "musical comedy" to the level of "comedy with music". The distinction, perhaps, is a trifle subtle; but a little reflection will show that it is not without significance. Unfortunately, Mr. Hall himself seems unable to realise its true meaning, for in attempting to soar to the heights of genuine wit he has only contrived to prove how dull a would-be humorist can be. Moreover, the old Adam is apparently still strong within him, as may be judged from much of the dialogue in *An Artist's Model*, which, on the first night at any rate, contained certain allusions that belong rather to the domain of the smart society paragraphist than to that of the witty epigrammatist. These defects, however, are of a kind which time and the exercise of a judicious self-restraint may cure; it is otherwise when one comes to the consideration of the many blemishes that disfigure the new piece as a dramatic work. In this respect Mr. Hall is evidently conscious of, and willing to acknowledge, his own deficiencies, inasmuch as he intimates in a footnote to the programme his indebtedness to Mr. James T. Tanner for assistance rendered in the construction of the comedy. What was the precise nature of the help afforded, the ordinary observer, perhaps, will have some difficulty in conceiving. For, as presented, *An Artist's Model* proved to be simply a mass of irrelevant details through which the main thread of the story could with difficulty be traced. Such being the case, it would be idle seriously to criticise a production so utterly devoid of proportion or dramatic significance, and of which the only redeeming features were the music, the lyrics, and the mounting. Mr. Sidney Jones's tuneful score deserved, in fact, a better fate than to be associated with so feeble a libretto; but, happily, he has discovered in Mr. Harry Greenbank a verse-writer worthy of collaboration with himself. Not only are Mr. Greenbank's lyrics humorous and neat, but they lend themselves admirably also to the composer's art, a circumstance of which Mr. Jones has taken the fullest advantage. An element of brightness was thus introduced into the performance which, without it, would have been lamentably dull and tedious. So poorly, also, has the author provided for his characters that, despite the exceptional strength of a talented and numerous company, few opportunities were afforded them of making an acting success. Miss Marie Tempest, however, whose return to the London stage is a welcome event, played and sang with marked ability; Miss Letty Lind's dancing was the delight of everyone; Miss Lottie Venne's arch and piquant manner proved of invaluable service; while Miss Leonora Braham, Mr. Eric Lewis, Mr. Yorke Stephens, Mr. Lawrence D'Orsay, and Mr. Blakeley struggled bravely to accomplish the impossible task of making bricks without straw. Nor was Mr. Hayden Coffin in much better case. So far as the music of his part is concerned, he showed himself as excellent an artist as ever; yet it is impossible to overlook the indifference, amounting almost to contemptuous carelessness, exhibited by his lackadaisical rendering of the hero's character. In all kindliness, Mr. Coffin must be counselled to change his method, or he will speedily lose what hold he possesses upon a public only too ready to show him every indulgence. It only remains to be added that the reception of the piece was of the stormiest description, and clearly indicated the feelings of dissatisfaction which its performance aroused in the audience.'

Edwardes set to work; the production was licked into shape and it ran in all 405 performances, an early example of critical dissatisfaction with a musical meaning little at the box office!

The romantic plot and the superior music were nearer comic or light opera than at the Gaiety, although once again modern contemporary fashion was largely used. The eventual outcome was 'a musical play', a description first used for *The Geisha*, the next production at Daly's in 1896. Whereas musical comedy had a slight farcical plot developed by the comedians and light singers, individual dancers and, of course, the girls, the musical play was built round a romantic plot of some substance, with a leading singer of ability appropriately supported by principals and chorus, the comedy being supplied by a comedian and a soubrette kept within bounds by the exigencies of the plot. Marie Tempest, from the world of light opera, Hayden Coffin, an excellent light baritone, Letty Lind as dancer and soubrette and Huntley Wright, an actor-comedian, set a pattern which many were to follow. So far chorus dancing except for the slightest graceful movement had little place in the new styles. These distinctions were to remain between the two theatres and were to be maintained by all the other managements who set up in the field of light musical entertainment until the nineteen-forties, when both styles became integrated under the American term the 'Musical'.

It is here we would like to point out that we have chosen for the book pictures of the stars of each era and scenes which, we hope, convey the style of each particular production. In the captions we have given the description which was used on the original programme. Changing tastes and methods of production have altered the status of many works and often managers and writers have aspired to designate pieces by the names of light opera or operette without sufficient justification.

Edwardes, with his usual eye on the box office, was later to reverse this process in 1907 by taking Viennese operetta and demoting it to English musical play, to add to the general confusion of style and description!

During the *fin de siècle*—the so-called Gay Nineties—while Edwardes was striving to consolidate musical comedy, he had, of course, competition from other managements, both old and new. These soon found writers and composers ready to join the ranks of purveyors of light entertainment fit for the Jubilee rejoicings and the anxious days of the Boer War at the end of the Victorian era.

[21]

William Greet had success with *Lord Tom Noddy* and *The Lady Slavey* and George Curzon was in 1901 to have, with *A Chinese Honeymoon*, the longest run of a musical piece to date; it ran at the Royal Strand Theatre for 1,075 performances.

In 1900 Seymour Hicks, who had left the Gaiety in 1897 and was now writing as well as acting, branched out on his own under the banner of the American manager, Charles Frohman, and with himself and his wife as the stars first opened at the Vaudeville Theatre. Tom B. Davis at the Lyric in 1899 with *Florodora* brought the names of Leslie Stuart and Paul Rubens to the fore and the chorus into prominence with the famous double sextet 'Tell me, pretty maiden'.

As if to mark the finish of an era the old Gaiety was pulled down for road improvements at the end of the run of *The Toreador* in 1903, though not before it had placed Ivan Caryll and Lionel Monckton among the principal composers of the hits of the day.

ACROSS THE ATLANTIC

On the other side of the water much the same pattern had been developing during the nineteenth century, founded on the first New York production of *The Beggar's Opera* in 1751.

Burletta, for which there was no legal need, and burlesque, for which there was no classical- or literary-minded public, did not have the same impact with the pioneers, and as the refugees and immigrants from the musically cultured European countries populated the States so a stronger light opera tradition asserted itself.

As in England the music hall became the entertainment of the working classes so in America the minstrel show developed and became the nation-wide entertainment of the masses. This mixture of negro and native talent, presented by white actors and singers 'blacked up', was the first unadulterated American entertainment devised and performed by native artists. When minstrelsy was imported to London it came, as a 'polite' middle-class musical entertainment, strangely free from the taint of vulgarity associated with the halls, and so contributed little to the development of musical comedy.

In America 'Music Hall' soon became 'Variety' or 'Vaudeville' (pronounced 'Vaw-der-vil') a mixture of every entertainment possible, since it was not fettered, as in England, by the licensing restrictions which until 1912 technically forbade spoken dialogue on the music-hall stage. One must not confuse burlesque in the English literal sense with American Burlesque (often called 'Bur-le-cue'), a low-class, twice-nightly, 'music-hall' strip-tease 'revue'.

It was the production in 1866 of *The Black Crook*, a fairy story extravaganza mixing ballet, operetta and spectacle, which set the pattern for the Broadway 'leg show' in which 'feminine pulchritude was shockingly revealed sans all Victorian modesty'. It ran 474 performances, was revived eight times and had toured up and down the country before the end of the century.

Then in 1868 the arrival from London of Lydia Thompson and her sensational 'British Blondes' with a burlesque company finally established the tradition of 'Glorifying the American show-girl'. The prudish Puritan opposition roused by these productions was soon able to turn with safety to Gilbert and Sullivan opera, both the imported and the native pirated versions.

A free style of topical, farcical, political entertainment, a kind of musical strip cartoon, was developed by Ned Harrigan and Tony Hart with David Brahams as composer. The first, *The Mulligans' Guard Ball* in 1879, was to be followed by twenty-three similar shows in the next seventeen years. In the eighties Gaiety burlesque was successfully exported by George Edwardes, but the American 'homespun' musicals like *My Sweetheart* seemed to be more successful in London than in New York.

The continental operetta and light-opera traditions, both imported and native, were becoming strongly embedded in the American musical theatre. Composers from the first- and second-generation expatriate Europeans played an important part in this development; many of these have not crossed the Atlantic or, if they have done so, it has been with little impact—just as many of our subsequent British lighter composers have not transplanted.

George Edwardes was quick to follow up his London successes with the new musical comedy and sent companies to Broadway, where *A Gaiety Girl*, 1893, *The Geisha*, 1896, and *A Runaway Girl*, 1898, soon established the style. At once the bulging-bosomed, broad-beamed amazons from the earlier days went the way of all flesh before the inrush of the Gaiety Girls in their long billowy skirts, dispensing charm and refinement. When *Florodora* was produced in New York in 1900, the six young ladies, the 'Pretty Maidens', achieved fame as the Florodora Sextette and made the American equivalent of Gaiety marriages into the peerage, becoming ladies of wealth and position in the Blue Book of American aristocracy.

The departure of Edwardes's *A Gaiety Girl* company for America was vividly described in the *Daily Telegraph* on 3 September 1894:

'With a few tears, an abundance of choice bouquets, the heartiest of cheers, and the sincerest of good wishes, Mr. George Edwardes's leading company bade farewell to London and to London playgoers on Saturday afternoon, and started on a twelve months' tour through the United States and Australia with *A Gaiety Girl*. A large crowd assembled at Waterloo Station to see them off by the boat-train for Southampton, where the popular artists embarked at seven o'clock on board the American liner *Berlin*, which is due at New York on Monday next. The company comprises Mr. Charles Ryley (who takes the part still played by Mr. C. Hayden Coffin at the Prince of Wales), Mr. Fred Kaye, Mr. W. Louis Bradfield, Mr. Cecil Hope, Mr. Leedham Bantock, Mr. E. J. Woodhouse, Mr. Fritz Rimma, Mr. Harry Monkhouse, Miss Decima Moore, Miss Sophie Elliot, Mrs. Edmund Phelps, Miss Blanche Massey, Miss Florence Lloyd, Miss Marie Yorke, Miss Grace Palotta, Miss Juliette Nesville, Miss Maud Hobson, Miss Ethel Selwyn, and Miss Fitzgerald, with Mr. Granville Bantock as musical director, and Mr. J. A. E. Malone, as manager. Many were the leave-takings on board before the steamer cast off at about eight o'clock, and many the congratulations bestowed upon Miss Decima Moore and Mr. Cecil Hope on their matrimonial engagement, the news of which became generally known on Saturday morning. Mr. George Edwardes, who, with Mr. Horace Lennard and others, accompanied the party down to Southampton, was the object of a little demonstration when the voyagers kissed their hands or waved their hats and handkerchiefs to him for the last time, the "Good-bye" taking the form of an appropriate adaptation of "Tommy Atkins" sung by the little group of actors and actresses from the upper deck of the vessel. On arrival in New York, *A Gaiety Girl* will have a week's rehearsal with its American chorus, and on the 17th will open at Daly's Theatre, where they will remain for two months. Visits will then be paid to Boston, Philadelphia, Chicago, Milwaukee, and other places en route for San Francisco. After a month's stay in the City of the Golden Gates, the company will take passage to Melbourne in the *Mariposa*, and before returning will halt at Sydney, Brisbane, and Adelaide. Negotiations are in progress for playing in India on the way home, but no arrangements have yet been concluded. In addition to *A Gaiety Girl* Mr. Malone has also taken with him *In Town*.'

The American operetta writers and composers were quick to seize on modern clothes and the new ideas and to create an amalgam which soon brought its successes. *The Belle of New York*, produced at the Casino Theatre, New York, in 1898, came to London with company, scenery and dresses the same year and ran for 697 performances. *The Era* said:

'In modern London the demand of playgoers is constantly for novelty; and the entertainment supplied by Mr. George W. Lederer's company from the Casino Theatre, New York, at the Shaftesbury Theatre on Tuesday last, 12 April, certainly meets the ever-present want. *The Belle of New York* is best described as *bizarre*. It is like nothing we have ever seen here, and it is composed of the oddest incongruities. Who—do our readers think—is the "belle" of the title? Some fashionable beauty of the whole or half world? No: it is a Salvation lassie. And be it remarked this fair Salvationist is by no means treated with contempt or ridicule. She is the heroine of the play—sweet, self-sacrificing, and sincere. But in this oddest of librettos self-sacrifice itself is eccentric. The Salvationist—though she breaks down and faints in the effort—actually appears, from the very best motives, in short skirts, and sings a slightly fast song in some public gardens where a fancy ball is being given. And with all this extravagance is mixed up a curious element of realism. The proceedings which recently followed an orgy of smart New Yorkers are effectively illustrated by the scene in *The Belle of New York*, where a rich young man, hopelessly intoxicated on his coming of age, contemplates his projected marriage, the next morning, with a queen of comic opera. Then we have streaks of local colour from low life, and the loves of a "mixed-ale pugilist" and a "Pell-street girl" are sketched for us not undivertingly. If we do not derive as much instruction as possible from seeing *The Belle of New York*, it is for want of explanation of some of the technical terms involved. A brief lexicon, printed on the programmes, would have conveyed to us what distinguishes the "mixed-ale pugilist" from the other varieties of his class, and also enlightened us as to the meaning of some of the more abstruse epithets employed by the characters in developing the story, which are quite new to most Londoners.

'Enjoyment of the style of Mr. Dan Daly, who plays Ichabod Bronson in *The Belle of New York*, is certainly an acquired taste; but once appreciated, his drollery is irresistible. The sepulchral, immovable manner in which he utters the most absurd remarks, and his extraordinary comic dancing combined with a Duke of Wellington profile and an eagle eye, constitute a combination of humours by which it is impossible not to be amused. His quaintness and drollery will be the talk in all Society circles.

'Mr. Harry Davenport gives a fresh, unaffected, and agreeable portrayal of the feather-brained Harry, and is likely to be popular with Shaftesbury audiences. Mr. J. E. Sullivan's study of lunacy, in his embodiment of Karl von Pumpernick, is so finished and clever as to be worthy of a real comedy. Mr. George K. Fortescue and Mr. George A. Schiller doubtless represent types of theatrical people who exist in the United States. We have nothing like them on this side of the Atlantic.

'Mr. Frank Lawton, whose appearances and manner as the "mixed-ale pugilist", are very characteristic, has wonderful talent as a whistler, and, in the second act, sends the audiences into raptures by his clear, sweet, long-sustained trillings. Mr. William H. Sloan and Mr. William Gould, made up exactly alike, represent twin Portuguese brothers in genuine burlesque style; and Mr. Edwin W. Hoff sings a patriotic song well as Billy Breeze, a sailor.

'Miss Edna May, who has a nice voice and uses it well, depicts the modest reserve of Violet Gray admirably; Miss Phyllis Rankin makes a dainty little Parisienne, and, as

Fifi Fricot, renders an arch ditty in the first act very neatly, her dance after leaving the bride-cake being one of the daintiest and prettiest things that we have seen on the stage for a long time. Miss Helen Dupont does justice to the dashing and unscrupulous character of Cora Angelique; Miss Mable Howe dances with much activity and vivacity as Kissie Fitzgarter; and Miss Hattie Moore represents Mamie Clancy, the "Pell-street girl", quite realistically.

'The chorus, who must have to do some hard work behind the scenes in changing, have plenty of spirit to spare for their business when on the stage, and do it most vigorously and smartly. The music is decidedly above average of musical play scores; indeed, the finale to the second act is over-elaborated for its purpose, and would gain by elisions. The scenery is effective and the dresses are decidedly bright and pretty. *The Belle of New York* is destined to be very popular, for it is the brightest, smartest, and cleverest entertainment of its kind that has been seen in London for a long time.'

Edna May was to remain in London and on the English stage, as did many later leading ladies from America. *The Belle of New York* was followed by other similar complete productions, *An American Beauty* and *The Casino Girl*, both in 1900.

In the States negro stage entertainment had developed from its own culture and music, which was later to blossom as Jazz, and the first all-negro musical comedy *In Dahomey*, produced in New York in 1903, came to London complete with company. Once again *The Era* reported:

'Negro entertainments in this country have been associated almost invariably with coon songs, cake-walks, and plantation walk-rounds. It is therefore a really fresh and novel experiment to introduce to the jaded Londoner an American musical comedy that is not only played throughout by real coloured people, but written and composed by clever and able representatives of the Negro race, with lyrics from the pen of a member of the same interesting nationality. The work of the composer, Mr. Will Marion Cook, stands out prominently in the entertainment; and on Saturday night in several of the numbers one could listen to excellent orchestration. Mr. Cook, who conducted with remarkable vigour and enthusiasm, is a pupil of Anton Dvořák, and in several of the concerted pieces in his score his music displays true dramatic perception. He is a most promising musician, who should shed a lustre on his race by work of a more solid and enduring character than is to be found in such a light and frankly frivolous production as *In Dahomey*. The remarkable thing about the whole entertainment on Saturday was the immense enthusiasm of the cast. Every member of the company—principals and chorus— sang and danced with a sense of thorough enjoyment of their work, and that enjoyment speedily communicated to the audience—which was both large and enthusiastic.

'*In Dahomey*, with its wonderful vitality, its quaint comedians, its catchy music, and its unique environment, should be one of the dramatic sensations of the London season.'

The two-way traffic of the stage was now assured—though many musicals suitable only for American consumption and vice versa were produced, and many 'nationalist' voices were to be raised on both sides complaining about 'foreign imports', little was now to change and each so-called innovation was to have its own distinctive impact on either side of the ocean.

Actors and actresses were to become transatlantic stars, but it was to be many years before the exchange of complete companies was again to take place, by which time the 'musical' had been born. Meantime an 'Equity' on both sides had begun firmly to hold the balance.

[25]

The post-Victorian and pre-war years, sometimes recalled as a long garden party, can almost be said, theatrically speaking, at least for the musical comedy, to have begun with the opening of the rebuilt Gaiety Theatre on its new site at the corner of the newly constructed Aldwych on 26 October 1903, in the presence of King Edward VII and Queen Alexandra in person. The new theatre, familiar faces and *The Orchid* ushered in eleven years of prosperity and the heyday of the picture-postcard beauty.

Edwardes had three main theatres under his banner, the Gaiety, Daly's and the Prince of Wales, besides intermittently putting on shows at the Lyric, the Adelphi and other theatres. Each theatre had its settled policy, the light-opera type of musical play at Daly's, midway musical comedy at the Prince of Wales and the more go-as-you-please style of piece at the Gaiety. His stars remained more or less fixed in their particular firmaments, but the lesser artists were moved from theatre to theatre as occasion demanded. Gertie Millar, Marie Studholme, Gabrielle Ray and Connie Ediss all epitomize Edwardesian Gaiety.

Other managements firmly established themselves. Seymour Hicks from the Vaudeville extended his activities to his own theatres, built for him by Charles Frohman, the Aldwych, 1905, and the Hicks (now the Globe), 1906. The Hicks's productions, with himself, Ellaline Terriss, the Dare sisters, Zena and Phyllis, Edna May, Camille Clifford and faces both old and new, set a fashionable style and provided rivals to the Gaiety Girls. Camille Clifford, who arrived in London with an American company playing *The Prince of Pilsen* in 1904, became the personification of American beauty as depicted in Charles Dana Gibson's drawings, which inspired the name of 'the Gibson Girls' in *The Catch of the Season*. In a similar way the daughters of Sir Timothy and Lady Bunn in *The Beauty of Bath* became 'the Bath Buns'.

George Curzon, who had been associated with Edwardes at the Prince of Wales, took over that theatre in 1907 and starred Isabel Jay, later his wife, who had graduated from the D'Oyly Carte company at the Savoy, in a series of musical plays mainly by Paul Rubens.

Robert Courtneidge, who came to London from provincial management and was a producer for Edwardes, launched out on his own at the Shaftesbury Theatre in 1909 with *The Arcadians*, the first of many productions, mostly specializing in realistic scenic effects on a grand scale, which continued until 1916. Florence Smithson, Cicely Courtneidge, Jack Hulbert, Harry Welchman, Iris Hoey, Dorothy Ward and Fay Compton were among those of his company who made their names.

At all these theatres the playgoer was certain to get a recognizable style of entertainment under whatever title fitted the moment. Plots moved freely all over the world, every unexpected corner of which was visited, Holland, Denmark, Ceylon, Persia, Japan, France and Germany all providing a locale. The past, the present and the future from Arcadia to Ruritania were traversed. The cinematograph and the aeroplane were exploited to provide new material for the books, all of which nevertheless remained inescapably English!

This was the period of the acceptance and integration of the American—especially if a millionaire—into English society, and players who had come over with visiting companies remained to star in London productions in the excellent parts the opportunity offered.

As yet dancing was mostly provided, with one or two exceptions, by principal 'exhibition dancers with a loosely contrived introduction into the plot, though a small dancing chorus was gradually used, the 'young ladies', or 'show-girls' as they became called in America, were only expected to move gracefully and stand around looking decorative. Later, popular ballroom dances, including the tango and the waltz, were exploited to the full on the musical stage.

By 1911 Revue was beginning to push Music Hall and Variety from their accepted haunts, the Empire, the Alhambra and the Hippodrome, taking the ballet associated with them into the new genre. The advent of the Russian dancers was felt only in revue. Similarly the new rhythms of Ragtime in 1912 had greater impact there than on the musical-comedy stage; a musical comedy, *Little Miss Ragtime*, achieved nothing more than a tour in 1913. The work of the new school of American composers was heard mainly in revue and as yet was seldom introduced into musical scores.

In such a period of prosperity the demand was bound to exceed the supply, and with so many rivals in the field George Edwardes was forced to seek abroad for fresh novelties and composers. He tried French light opera at Daly's with little success, and in 1906 J. A. E. Malone, Edwardes's manager and right-hand man, was searching the Continent for new ideas. He saw in Vienna a new operetta, *Die Lustige Witwe* by Franz Lehár, which contained the essence of traditional Viennese music with a contemporary chic plot set in Paris. Malone was enthusiastic and persuaded a rather reluctant Edwardes to go and see it. Still unenthusiastic, he bought the rights, thinking it might prove a six week stop-gap. An English book was prepared, turning the operetta into a musical play, *The Merry Widow*, building up the comedy, scoring down the music and making a new third act at Maxime's. He cast Lily Elsie, who had been on the musical stage in London since *A Chinese Honeymoon* and later in his own productions, as the Widow, and Joe Coyne, an American light comedian, who insisted he was not a romantic lover or singer, as Danilo. He added his stock comedians W. H. Berry and George Graves with Robert Evett and Elizabeth Firth to provide the romantic vocal power. The result produced on 8 June 1907 was a tremendous success which set London waltzing and the ladies wearing the fashionable large feathered hat. It made the names of its stars remembered to this present day and set the fashion for Viennese operetta which was to stay until the outbreak of the war in 1914 caused a temporary eclipse.

After *The Merry Widow*, which ran for 778 performances, came *The Dollar Princess*, 1909, *The Count of Luxembourg*, 1911, *Gipsy Love*, 1912 and *The Marriage Market*, 1913, all at Daly's. *The Waltz Dream* (first at the Hicks in 1908 and revived at Daly's in 1911) and other Viennese works like *A Chocolate Soldier* which followed in the wake of the success of *The Merry Widow* unashamedly called themselves operettas and so have no place in this chronicle.

Side by side the English composer and his continental cousin ruled the musical stage until the gaiety of nations was dimmed and cultural barriers erected in August 1914.

THE WAR YEARS

An excess of patriotic zeal was to clear the stage of German artists and productions, and as if symbolically George Edwardes was caught by surprise at the outbreak of war on a 'cure' at Bad Nauheim and was interned by the Germans. His health broken, he was repatriated, but lived only until 4 October 1915. At his death his affairs were in an almost bankrupt state.

It was Robert Evett who took control at Daly's and not only piloted the estate into complete solvency but allowed the Edwardes family to make a substantial fortune when they eventually sold out in 1922. The Gaiety was bought by Alfred Butt and run on traditional lines by George Grossmith and Edward Laurillard.

The first production of the Evett régime was *A Happy Day* (1916); its predecessor, *Betty*, had been planned under Edwardes himself. It brought to Daly's José Collins, but it was the next production, *The Maid of the Mountains* in 1917, which established her as the queen of the musical stage when it started its run of 1,352 performances.

At the Gaiety *To-Night's the Night* (1915), with a Paul Rubens score, had two Jerome Kern numbers interpolated: 'They didn't believe me' and 'Any old night'. Its successor, *Theodore and Co.*, was a collaboration musically of Ivor Novello and Kern and made the name of Leslie Henson; in the same way a completely American 'Aviation' musical comedy, *Going Up*, which followed, established Evelyn Laye. The new generation of composers both English and American were knocking at the door and making themselves heard.

At the Shaftesbury in 1916 Courtneidge at the end of his reign was featuring the younger players Noël Coward and the Hulberts (Jack and Cicely, now married) in *The Light Blues*, and Phyllis Dare, now a leading lady in her own right, at the Adelphi made a big success with a violin song in *Tina*. Following this at the Adelphi a strange phenomenon was to be seen: the leading-lady star, with her usual able and romantic support, had been supplanted by a comedian at the top of the bill. W. H. Berry, the first comedian since Arthur Roberts, at the very commencement of this story, starred in *High Jinks* in 1916, which was followed by *The Boy* (1917) and *Who's Hooper?* (1919), remaining at this theatre, almost continually, till 1923 under Alfred Butt's management.

The gradual change that was coming over light music was eventually to divide sharply the romantic from what was to become jazz and syncopation, and although revue, one of the most popular of war-time entertainments, helped to establish their rhythms, the musical-comedy world was not completely immune to the new sound.

Two extremely opposed productions were to be the most remembered of war-time musicals apart from *The Maid of the Mountains*. First *The Bing Boys are Here*, technically calling itself a revue or 'A picture of London in seven panels', had more or less continuous, though episodic, story lines and may be considered a musical comedy. It was derived from a French original, but thoroughly Anglicized for the Alhambra in 1916. It brought its principal artists, George Robey, Alfred Lester and Violet Loraine from revue and the halls, and with its successors, *The Bing Girls are There* (1917) and *The Bing Boys on Broadway* (1918), gave songs to the army on the march: 'If you were the only girl in the world', 'Let the great big world keep turning' and 'First love, lost love, best love'. An imitation, *The Other Bing Boys*, a Jewish version at the London Opera House in 1917, did not achieve such fame.

The second success, *Chu Chin Chow*, an Arabian Nights fairy-tale extravaganza, a *Forty Thieves* pantomime without the usual pantomime irrelevances, was turned by Oscar Asche with Frederic Norton's music into what was almost light opera. Spectacularly staged and dressed, or undressed, in a style 'more navel than millinery', as remarked by Lady Tree! It gave the bleak war years from 1916, well into the almost as bleak first peace years up to 1920, a glamorous escape into a romantic alien world of make-believe. Its 2,238 performances at His Majesty's Theatre were not surpassed by a musical until *Salad Days* was the first to break its record many years later. (For a list of long runs see page 40.)

When peace came in 1918 much had been swept away, ideas had changed and a new

[28]

morality was established—even though Shaw's Eliza Doolittle had said 'bloody' in April 1914 before it all started! Old managements had gone, old favourites had died or retired, and the stage was cleared for the brave new world.

THE GAY TWENTIES

As the new decade dawned everyone expected and was resignedly prepared for the Americanization of the world fit for heroes. Had not the great Enrico Caruso made a gramophone record of a patriotic war song by that most American and parochial of Yankee Doodle Dandies, George M. Cohan, to warn us 'Over there—the Yanks are coming over there'?

Jazz made its appearance on the stage in the person of the Original Dixieland Band in the revue *Joy-Bells* at the Hippodrome in 1919. The sound of the trumpet, the saxophone, the ukelele, the banjolele and the drums were to take their place in the orchestra pit, together with the syncopated pianist, while pianos—one, two or three—were later sometimes used alone to provide the accompaniment.

As yet the musical stage had not felt the full impact of the American language, though gangster plays in the legitimate theatre had often to have glossaries printed in the programmes when plays came over or all-American casts appeared. It was not until the advent of the 'talkies' in 1929 at the end of this era that the full significance of the American voice was revealed.

The peace year of 1919 saw the conversion of the Middlesex Music Hall, which Stoll had rebuilt in 1911 with little success, into the Winter Garden Theatre under the management of Grossmith and Laurillard. Their first production, *Kissing Time*, had music by one of the old guard, Ivan Caryll, and a book by Guy Bolton and P. G. Wodehouse, just beginning to make their international names as musical-comedy writers; although English, both were settled in America at this period. *Kissing Time* had started life in America the previous year as *The Girl Behind the Gun*, but was rewritten for London.

This process of revising for the London stage, even though the leading artists were often from the States, was to be the practice throughout the twenties, when the importation of American shows was at its peak.

Kissing Time, with Phyllis Dare, Yvonne Arnaud, Leslie Henson, Stanley Holloway, Tom Walls and Grossmith himself, couldn't have been more English, in spite of Yvonne Arnaud, then still a musical-comedy star! Another Bolton-Wodehouse book with a Jerome Kern score, *Oh, Boy!* in New York, became *Oh, Joy!* in London, with Beatrice Lillie at the Kingsway Theatre.

The mixture as before continued both at the Adelphi with W. H. Berry and with José Collins at Daly's, although she was to move to the Gaiety in 1922 for *The Last Waltz* and her decline. Phyllis Dare took her place at Daly's with *The Lady of the Rose*, but the day of the romantic, Ruritanian continental musical play was waning.

The new trend in the lighter musical comedies was towards dancing. Ziegfeld in New York had glorified the show-girl and had taught his chorus to dance. In London, John Tiller-trained troupes like the Palace Girls had remained in variety and revue. It was left to the Americans to coin the phrase 'Bring on the Girls' used by producers whenever the dialogue or the piece showed signs of sagging. This was to become as useful as Ducrow's 'Cut the cackle and come to the 'osses' had been in similar circumstances in the equestrian drama one hundred years earlier. As yet a ballet training had not become a necessity for the dancers, although on occasions now they were sometimes required to 'go up on their points'.

The new stars were dancers as well as singers. Dorothy Dickson, with her husband Caryl Hyson, came to London in 1921 as exhibition dancers in revue. She remained to become the leading lady at the Winter Garden in *Sally* (1921); in which she had even had to cope with 'The Butterfly Ballet' to the interpolated music of Victor Herbert in a Jerome Kern score. She was to be at the Winter Garden in similar productions, *The Cabaret Girl* (1922), *The Beauty Prize* (1924) and *Tip Toes* (1926), a Gershwin score. The Astaires came to London with *Stop Flirting* at the Shaftesbury Theatre in 1923 and brought a new dimension to musical comedy. They sang and danced through the twenties with *Lady Be Good* (1926) and *Funny Face* (1928) to the music of George Gershwin, who was to become established as the high priest of jazz.

So many American writers, composers and artists were now in London that often the new shows had their genesis in this country. *Primrose* was written and produced at the Winter Garden in 1924, the first Gershwin score in London. A strange reversal of the usual procedure now happened: Gertrude Lawrence, who had made her name in revue on both sides of the Atlantic, remained in New York to star in Gershwin's new *Oh, Kay* with an American cast in 1926; she came back to her native London with the show the following year at His Majesty's with an English company, after being the first English leading lady to create an American musical on Broadway.

Of other English stars Jack Buchanan and Jack Hulbert were making their names both singing and dancing the new tap routines (derived from what had originally been called 'clog dancing' in the previous century), and the whole chorus had to follow the lead and the beat. June, who, as June Tripp, had been one of Pavlova's 'Snowflakes', combined song and ballet and was in demand as 'the love interest'.

Daly's, under its new manager, James White, found a new leading lady in Evelyn Laye with *Madame Pompadour* (1923), which was in the old continental tradition, but soon both Daly's and the Gaiety had to fall back on revivals, *The Merry Widow*, *The Dollar Princess* and *The Shop Girl*. Even old Gaiety burlesque, *Faust on Toast*, was tried with complete disaster. By the end of the twenties Daly's was but a name, the tradition had gone. The Gaiety however was to find itself again. A series of musical comedies with an established team including Stanley Lupino, Laddie Cliff, Phyllis Monckman, Cyril Ritchard and Madge Elliott took it safely into the early nineteen-thirties.

An oasis in the desert of shifting sounds was provided by *Lilac Time*, which brought Courtice Pounds, an old Savoy favourite, to Schubert and to stardom at the Lyric Theatre in 1922; it was revived four times in the decade.

In 1925 London saw the first of the new large-scale American musicals, *Rose Marie*, the product of the literary writer, operetta style composer and spectacular producer. Ziegfeld had staged this with Mary Ellis in New York in 1924; and for the production at Drury Lane, Edith Day, who once before had come to this country in *Irene* at the Empire in 1920, returned to play the lead. The Theatre Royal, Drury Lane, since its interior rebuilding in 1922 had presented almost one failure after another, remaining true to its tradition of the spectacular drama and pantomime, but when *Rose Marie* opened on 20 March the theatre's future was assured for the next seven years, even the regular pantomime had to be almost completely dropped. 'The Indian Love Call', the Totem Dance with its drilled dancing chorus and the Mounties, and equally well-drilled singers, all set new standards which were followed by *The Desert Song* (1927), *Show Boat* (1928) and *New Moon* (1929).

Rudolf Friml and Sigmund Romberg as composers with Oscar Hammerstein II led the field. The books became stronger and stronger; old plays became musicals. *If I were King* became *The Vagabond King* (1927) and *Old Heidelberg* became *The Student Prince*; incidentally called a light opera, it strangely had two unsuccessful London productions in 1926 and 1929, but lived 'on tour', and had its longest West End run in 1968–9. *No, No, Nanette* and *Betty in Mayfair* both started life as plays, and *Show Boat* brought Edna Ferber's novel to the musical stage.

The musical-comedy centres had shifted. The London Hippodrome deserted revue for successes like *Mercenary Mary* (1925), *Sunny* (1926), *Hit the Deck* (1927), *That's a Good Girl* (1928). New theatres were built; the Carlton opened with *Lady Luck* in 1927, the Piccadilly opened with *Blue Eyes* in 1928, the Dominion, far too large ever to get a real success, opened with *Follow Through* in 1929, and at the end of the decade the London Casino started its life as the Prince Edward, with *Rio Rita* in 1930. After checkered careers all these were to become cinemas either intermittently or permanently by the time of the 'talkies' boom in the early thirties.

Perhaps the musical comedy most associated with the twenties is *No, No, Nanette*; the songs 'Tea for Two' and 'I want to be happy' seem to bestride the decade. A failure on tour in the States, it was produced in London at the Palace Theatre and later became a success in New York. Its stars, two middle-aged old favourites, George Grossmith and Joe Coyne, Binnie Hale brimming with youth and vitality and Irene Brown to sing the blues, were to carry the show through 668 performances, and this theatre also forsook revue to become the home of musical comedies for many years to come. During the twenties *Princess Charming* (1926) Anglicized Viennese, *The Girl Friend*, an early Richard Rogers and Lorenz Hart collaboration, *Virginia* (1928) (the song 'Roll away clouds' suited the mood of the period) and *Dear Love* (1929) were some other Palace hits.

The move over into the thirties saw little change; the pattern had been set by the vintage years of 1925–6 and there was now nothing very new to come on the entertainment scene, only the crackle and squeak of the early 'talkies'. The celluloid backstage land of Broadway was enticing patrons away from live entertainment. What would be the result on the box office and on touring? Musicians who feared 'canned' music asked the vital questions. Though much the same fear was felt over the threat of the wireless when it came earlier in the decade, it had been made to help rather than hinder the theatre, although variety and music hall suffered irrecoverably.

There was no need to panic; the new Palace musical was called *Hold Everything*, and Noël Coward had produced his first full-length musical *Bitter-Sweet* at His Majesty's.

THE TURBULENT THIRTIES

The threat of the 'talkies' at the beginning of the thirties and the impending reality of war, which hung over the later years, made for a disturbed decade.

The 'talkies' hit the provincial and outlying theatres and the variety world most of all, but the West End either drew in its horns or set out to compete with the new menace and, as it always does with any 'new' invention, learned to live with it.

Charles B. Cochran, who had made his name with revues in the twenties as the most fastidious of producers, was probably the only man of great artistic integrity in the field of light theatre to work in this country. He employed directors, writers, dancers, artists and designers of the front rank for his productions. He sponsored Noël Coward from his early years, and after *Bitter-Sweet* in 1929, was responsible for *Conversation Piece* in 1934.

His financial ups and downs were symptomatic of the between-wars period.

Cochran's *Ever Green*, which reopened a rebuilt Adelphi Theatre in 1930, had some ten designers to bring it to life on the stage, with Jessie Matthews and Sonnie Hale as its stars. *Nymph Errant* in 1933 will always be remembered for Gertrude Lawrence, Elizabeth Welch and its Cole Porter score.

Oswald Stoll, who had made his name as a purveyor of artistic variety for family audiences at the Coliseum and the Alhambra, now found his public drifting away from those large houses. He lured them back with lavish Germanic productions in which anything might happen and the whole theatre could become involved when the production spilled over into the audience, while the stage revolved in several directions. *White Horse Inn* (1931) and *Casanova* (1932) among others brought success to the Coliseum and *Waltzes from Vienna* did the same for the Alhambra, in 1931.

This great outlay was balanced by the growth of the small intimate comedy with music but no chorus, just a simple story with songs, often an old farce revamped. Bobby Howes at the Saville and Leslie Henson at the Strand had their successes with this new form.

Drury Lane was not to keep up its reputation made in the twenties. The day of the American musical play was waning and it took Ivor Novello to combine the old traditional autumn melodrama and romantic operetta, à la Lehár, in *Glamorous Night* in 1935. Even after this had saved the Lane's exchequer the management would not give Novello a second chance until, after another bad period, they had to beg him to return in triumph with *Careless Rapture*. He remained until the war shut the theatre and *The Dancing Years* temporarily closed.

The Gaiety had a successful twilight; it was finally condemned in February 1939 and demolished in 1957. After the popular light musical comedies with Laddie Cliff and Stanley Lupino there eventually followed a series of musical comedies, under Firth Shepherd's management, usually having Vivian Ellis as composer, with Leslie Henson, Fred Emney and Richard Hearne. *Seeing Stars* (1935), *Swing Along* (1936), *Going Greek* (1937) and *Running Riot* (1938) are titles which convey the style.

Strangely, once again some London theatres had become established with a recognizable style of entertainment in these pre-war years. The Hippodrome, the Saville and the Palace had their settled stars during this decade: Jack Hulbert and Cicely Courtneidge, Bobby Howes and Binnie Hale, Arthur Riscoe and Frances Day, Jack Buchanan and Elsie Randolph, all headed the bills in the mixture as before.

Broadcasts from the theatres themselves, started in the twenties, had helped to unite the media. The gramophone, particularly since electric recordings appeared in 1925, had also brought the stars and their songs right into the home. Curiously, Edwardes had been suspicious of the gramophone in its early years and had not allowed his artists or productions to be recorded if he could prevent it. Today the first thing to be done is to get the L.P. album of a new musical on the market!

On the whole, theatrical fare was very English as far as the musical stage was concerned, leaving America to the 'talkies'. The biggest change of direction in the period was to be found in *On Your Toes* by Rodgers and Hart, a show from America that brought real ballet to the musical-comedy stage both in its backstage plot and in performers. It had Vera Zorina as its leading lady. The Ballanchine Ballet, 'Slaughter on Tenth Avenue', paved the way for the musicals of the forties and fifties, but the production did not run in London despite a gallant reprieve by the company at the Coliseum after it had to leave the Palace. It was before its time, though copied in part by its contemporaries.

Me and My Girl in 1937 at the Victoria Palace was very much of its time; a coronation romp, it made history with 'The Lambeth Walk', which ran or danced on into the days of the blackout and the roaring forties.

THE SECOND WAR YEARS

The closure of the theatres at the outbreak of the war was of short duration and during the phoney war, before the 'blitz', established successes like *The Dancing Years* returned to the West End—at the Adelphi, as Drury Lane had become the headquarters of E.N.S.A.— and ran for 969 performances. Novello was to have two other wartime shows, *Arc de Triomphe* at the Phoenix in 1943 and *Perchance to Dream* at the Hippodrome in 1945.

London saw two Cole Porter musicals, *Du Barry was a Lady* at His Majesty's in 1942 and *Panama Hattie* at the Piccadilly in 1943, but the main musical-comedy fare was provided when the theatres were open (between 'blitz' and 'doodle bug') by many revivals of past and tried favourites. London again saw *Chu Chin Chow*, Palace 1940; *White Horse Inn*, Coliseum 1942; *The Maid of the Mountains*, Coliseum 1942; *Rose Marie*, Stoll 1942; *The Belle of New York*, Coliseum 1942; *Lilac Time*, Stoll 1942; *Wild Rose* (a revised version of *Sally*), Princes 1942; *The Merry Widow*, His Majesty's 1943; *Show Boat*, Stoll 1943; *The Vagabond King*, Winter Garden 1943; *The Desert Song*, Prince of Wales 1943; *The Quaker Girl*, Coliseum 1944, and *Irene*, His Majesty's 1945. Many others were seen 'on tour' only. More original work was done and reputations made in revue both topical and spectacular.

Of English light musicals, the Hulberts provided topical examples at the Palace and Lupino Lane at the Victoria Palace kept the flag flying. One of the more serious efforts, *The Lisbon Story* at the Hippodrome, broke new ground with an up-to-date spy story in which the leading lady was killed by the time the curtain fell.

Generally speaking, we had lost touch with Broadway, which itself had been resting on its laurels for some time. The hectic war years on both sides were, theatrically speaking, a calm before the storm.

ENTER THE MUSICAL

In the latter days of the war rumours reached London of a great new change which had come over the Broadway musical stage, almost overnight, on 31 March 1943, with the production of *Oklahoma!*

This venture of an artistic play-producing company, the Theatre Guild, was based on a dramatic play, *Green Grow the Lilacs* by Lynn Riggs, which had not been a spectacular success when produced some years earlier. The music was by Richard Rodgers, lately sundered from his partner Lorenz Hart, now teamed with Oscar Hammerstein II, whose great record of successes in the twenties had become slightly dimmed in later years. An essential part of the new collaboration was provided by Agnes de Mille, the dancer and choreographer, whose work was to electrify London at Covent Garden with the New York Ballet Theatre before we even saw *Oklahoma!*

The preparation of the new musical play—the new generic term Musical did not make its appearance until about 1950—took place in great secrecy and an atmosphere of predicted failure. There was not a box-office name in the cast to help it, but it ran 2,278 performances, setting up a Broadway record beaten only by *My Fair Lady* and *Hello, Dolly!*

A New York historian of musical comedy, Jack Burton, in his *The Blue Book of Broadway Musicals* (1952) says:

'This phenomenal production set a new pattern for girl-and-music shows in which every line, every song, every dance routine is an indispensable part of a closely knit whole. It was a show that had dramatic substance and never ran off the plot track, and so real, so simple, so engrossing was its story that its narration could be safely entrusted to other than big name stars.

'This was a formula that called for meticulous craftsmanship and a passion for perfection with which both Richard Rodgers and Oscar Hammerstein II are uncommonly gifted. Hammerstein especially is a slave to accuracy. He took measurements in the Philadelphia zoo and a field of tasselled maize before writing 'The corn grows as high as an elephant's eye', and talked with chowder cooks to make sure there would be no culinary mistake in the lyrics he wrote for 'This is a real nice clambake'. And Rodgers and Hammerstein held fast to these high ideals in the later musicals on which they collaborated.'

At last ballet was an integral part of the plot; in the dream sequence the leading characters were 'doubled' by dancers, making it a complete work of art.

London had to wait four years to see another 'rebirth' of musical comedy arrive from across the Atlantic. Meantime Drury Lane reopened with Noël Coward's *Pacific 1860* in December 1946. Cochran, on his feet again, presented an A. P. Herbert and Vivian Ellis musical play, *Big Ben*, at the Adelphi (1946), and followed this with *Bless the Bride* in April 1947, which made the name of Lizbeth Webb and had a long run. Four days later *Oklahoma!* opened at Drury Lane and started on its run of 1,543 performances. Once again a complete American production with company was in London. Its impact repeated that of its New York première. Old values were changed, new training was needed for actors, singers and dancers. The whole musical-comedy world from the manager's office to the stage door had to be on its toes, if it was to be with the new trends.

Irving Berlin's *Annie Get Your Gun* had a stupendous opening at the Coliseum later the same year and these theatres were to hear the scores of American musicals for some years to come. His Majesty's with *Brigadoon* in 1949 was to follow the capitulation on Broadway. Only at the Palace with *King's Rhapsody* (1949) did Novello provide a triumphant swan song for Ruritania and the world of operetta.

The full circle of the new style was completed when the musical became indivisible from ballet, with *West Side Story* (Her Majesty's, 1958). Conceived by a dancer and choreographer, Jerome Robbins, and composed by Leonard Bernstein from the world of classical music, it approached the whole form from another angle, proved its success and provided lessons to be learned in all quarters.

The London theatre in the fifties fluctuated between American stars and companies in complete carbon-copy reproductions of Broadway, and the home-grown efforts now learned that a strong book was a necessity and that good ballet dancing had its place. Old plays one after another were made into musicals: *Blue for a Boy* (*It's a Boy*), His Majesty's 1950; *Zip Goes a Million* (*Brewster's Millions*), Palace 1951; *Love from Judy* (*Daddy Long-Legs*), Saville 1950, all were successes. Even J. M. Barrie provided the plot for *Dear Miss Phoebe* (*Quality Street*), Phoenix 1950, and *Wild Grows the Heather* (*The Little Minister*), Hippodrome 1956.

The two phenomena of 1954 were *Salad Days*, written as an end-of-season romp, by Dorothy Reynolds and Julian Slade for the Bristol Old Vic Company, which unexpectedly became a record runner at the Vaudeville, and *The Boy Friend*, a brilliant nostalgic pastiche of the 1920s by Sandy Wilson which, after two tentative starts at the Players' Theatre, settled in for 2,084 performances at Wyndham's Theatre. New stars appeared, were made overnight, only to vanish from the theatre. Television had come to stay and proved an all-devouring monster for stage talent, to say nothing of audiences; but in spite of much drawing-in of horns in many directions the threat of the 'box' has proved no more worrying to the West End than that of wireless and the 'talkies'. All have settled down to live amicably together, though touring and the provinces have suffered greatly. The biggest enemy turned out to be tax restrictions, changing incomes and the general shift-round of social values, together with rising production costs: all a question of economics. Long runs became necessary if expenditure was to show a profit; in fact, the four longest runs of the London musical stage were all achieved after 1954.

Directors who had made their names in the field of the drama turned to the musical stage with equal success. Peter Brook's *Irma La Douce* (Lyric, 1958) was a landmark in staging, as was the work of Joan Littlewood, which went through the London theatre like a dose of salts. Gradually English composers recovered and learned from the American invasion. Lionel Bart's *Oliver!* (New, 1960) met the challenge and crossed the Atlantic to redress the balance somewhat. Theatrically in the decade London was to conquer Broadway with its new plays and actors.

By the end of the fifties the whole structure of star-casting new musicals was to change. They needed actors and actresses who could sing and if necessary dance. No longer could the singer or dancer, who could only just act, get away with parts as written. Musical needs were to become subservient to dramatic values. New stars were to come from the legitimate theatre or had to be found and trained in the new techniques. Gradually the acting profession has become one again, no longer is it 'straight' and 'musical', though a few leading ladies in the twenties like Gertrude Lawrence and Dorothy Dickson had managed to star in both worlds.

Together with the vanishing of revue as a form of entertainment in the mid-sixties, and the death of live variety and music hall in the accepted sense of the word, the 'performer' has drifted back to his original haunts, the public house and the club, particularly in the provinces, making up with the 'pop' singer what is now referred to as 'show business'.

There has arisen a difficulty with the younger actors trained in the theatre of today with their built-in aversion to long runs. Unfortunately these are necessary to offset the modern vast expenditure on a new production. Often also actors' sights are set on the subsidized theatre and its changing repertoire. How this is to be resolved is a problem for the seventies.

The excessive costs of mounting productions in America gave birth to the off-Broadway theatre where productions of artistic merit but of dubious commercial possibilities, at least to the Broadway producer, could be initially tried out on a small scale and new experiments made. Both *Man of La Mancha*, Piccadilly, 1958, and *Hair*, Shaftesbury (the Princes re-named), 1968, belong to this class. The former, a complete fusion of music and drama allied to dancing and direction, raising the musical to near operatic level, and the latter, with its up-to-the-minute rhythms, topicality and advanced staging, may yet blaze a trail for the future or prove sterile in its own brilliance, as did the revue *Beyond the Fringe*. Only the seventies will show.

W. A. Darlington's farewell criticism for *The Daily Telegraph*, was, ironically enough as it happened, of *Hair*—produced on 28 September 1968, the evening after the jurisdiction of the Lord Chamberlain had ended and theatrical censorship ceased. While giving it a bad notice initially, he later explained his feelings in the course of a reflective article 'Pride in Prejudice', after it had established itself as a success:

'I make no apology, you may notice, for my prejudice. Ideally speaking, perhaps, a critic shouldn't have any; but if any human being were to succeed in arriving at such a state of balance he would be so mild a character that nobody would pay any attention to his opinions anyway. All the critic can do about his prejudices is to recognize them for what they are and let his readers know about them.

'James Agate, for example, was quite furiously prejudiced against musicals, and also against any form of fantasy: but he took care to warn his public of both these aberrations —even to the point, if my memory serves me, of admitting that his opinion on these matters was not worth having.'

This leads to the age-long controversy, now more urgently than ever in need of solution. The dramatic critic is expected to cover the field of the music and ballet critics. He naturally can only concern himself with the plot and dramatic values. On the other hand, a music critic is far too 'highbrow' for any appreciation of light music, even to the extent of deploring its existence in his own rarefied world of the opera house, and he naturally is not acclimatized to the niceties of the art of acting.

As things are at present, whichever is sent to a musical he must be left uncomfortably standing in the aisle of criticism, not seated on either side. Generally speaking, the result is a bad notice. Critics of a new breed must make their appearance who can find their seats placed firmly and comfortably in the aisle and report, as it were, from both sides of the gangway.

This is, of course, all-important to the manager, and he is often forced to go to inordinate lengths to counter any influence the critics may have on his particular public. A vast publicity machine is therefore brought into action and can sometimes save the day.

Musical comedy was born and bred in the era of the totally commercial theatre and has remained its greatest surviving prop to this day. And who should raise a voice to say that this should not be so while theatre lives? Though it may seem strange in this context to invoke the managerial voice of Irving, it is in personal interviews given in America, where the art of the reporter was 'invented', that we find (though he is naturally talking of the legitimate drama) what must and should always be the managerial creed and the final judgement by which a musical must stand or fall in the theatre today.

'However successful art may be,' he said, 'its true value as applied to the drama can only be determined by public appreciation.'

He made very clear that audience approval was the sole arbiter not only of acting but of every aspect of production. For instance, his selection of play scripts was the inevitable result of the uninformed public opinion of the day.

He also added: 'The managers cannot force upon the public either very good or very bad plays. They (the managers) haven't got the power.'—All he lacked was the foreknowledge of the powers of publicity! Thus speaks the self-styled humble servant of the public in 1883, 163 years after Dr. Johnson had written these lines for Garrick to speak:

'The drama's laws the drama's patrons give,
For we that live to please, must please to live.'

1. *Left*. Fathers of Musical Comedy, 1893. Owen Hall (Jimmy Davis), George Edwardes and Sidney Jones.

2. *Lower left*. Arthur Roberts as Captain Coddington in *In Town*, a musical farce by Adrian Ross and James Leader, music by Osmond Carr, Prince of Wales Theatre, 1892.

3. *Below*. Topsy Sinden as Eva, an Ambiguity Girl, in the second edition of *In Town*, Gaiety Theatre, 1893.

4. *Left*. Alfred C. Seymour and Letty Lind as Vivian and the Hon. Maude Sportington in *Morocco Bound*, a musical farcical comedy by Arthur Branscombe, lyrics by Adrian Ross, music by Osmond Carr, Shaftesbury Theatre, 1893.

5. *Lower left*. Fritz Rimma and Rutland Barrington in the bathing machine scene with Miss Warden, from *A Gaiety Girl*, a musical comedy by Owen Hall, lyrics by Harry Greenbank, music by Sidney Jones, during the latter part of its run at the Prince of Wales Theatre which started in 1893.

6. *Below*. Hayden Coffin as Charles Goldfield, Captain in the IX Life Guards, in *A Gaiety Girl*. His song 'Private Tommy Atkins' was one of the successes of the period.

7. *Right*. Ada Reeve as Bessie Brent in *The Shop Girl*, a musical farce by H. J. W. Dam, music by Ivan Caryll, Gaiety Theatre, 1894.
The Charity Bazaar:
   'Basket included, thirty pounds'
   'Isn't that a little warm?'
   'They're hot-house flowers, Sir.'

8. *Above.*
'Foundlings are we,
Waiting to see,
Who will unravel our pre-natal mystery.'
A group of George Edwardes's Gaiety Girls in
The Shop Girl.

9. *Left.* 'And I'm the Johnny who trots 'em round . . .' George Grossmith as Bertie Boyd, 'Beautiful Bountiful Bertie', in *The Shop Girl.*
'And please to note that the cut of my coat is quite the thing.'

10. *Above.* Ellaline Terriss singing 'A Simple Little String' in *The Circus Girl*, a musical play by James T. Tanner and W. Palings, lyrics by Harry Greenbank and Adrian Ross, music by Ivan Caryll and Lionel Monckton, Gaiety Theatre, 1896.

'Make him put his slippers on
And be sure his boots are gone
And you've got him on a string, you see.'

11. *Above right.* Seymour Hicks as Dick Capel and Ellaline Terriss as Dora Wemyss in *The Circus Girl*.

'I envy the man with the dogs who perform
And give themselves airs when waltzing in pairs.'

12. *Right.* May Yohe as Phyllis in *The Lady Slavey*, a musical comedy by George Dance, music by John Crook, Avenue Theatre, 1894.

'He isn't going to fancy me, I s'pose?
But he might—one never knows.'

13. *Above left*. Marie Tempest as Adèle in *An Artist's Model*, a comedy with music by Owen Hall, lyrics by Harry Greenbank, music by Sidney Jones, Daly's Theatre, 1895.

14. *Above*. Marie Tempest as O Mimosa San in *The Geisha*, a Japanese musical play by Owen Hall, lyrics by Harry Greenbank, music by Sidney Jones, Daly's Theatre, 1896.

15. *Left*. Mabel Love as Nurse Phoebe in *Lord Tom Noddy*, a musical piece by George Dance, music by Osmond Carr, Garrick Theatre, 1896. The title role was played by Little Tich brought from the music halls.

16. *Above*. Lillie Belmore as Mrs Honeycomb, Frank Wheeler as Auguste Pompier, Lionel Rignold as Ebenezer Honeycomb and Ada Reeve as Julie Bon-Bon in *The Gay Parisienne*, a musical comedy by George Dance, music by Ivan Caryll, Duke of York's Theatre, 1896.

17. *Right*. Louie Freear as Ruth singing 'Sister Mary Jane's Top Note' in *The Gay Parisienne*.
   'Sit back! Hold tight! Mary's going to sing!
   She's going to try again to crack her throat!'

18. *Above left.* Gaiety Girls, Lady Coodle's party in *A Runaway Girl*, a musical comedy by Seymour Hicks and Harry Nicholls, lyrics by Aubrey Hopwood and Harry Greenbank, music by Ivan Caryll and Lionel Monckton, Gaiety Theatre, 1898.

19. *Far left.* Edmund Payne as Flipper in *A Runaway Girl*.

20. *Left.* Arthur Roberts as *Gentleman Joe* (*The Hansom Cabby*) a musical farce by Basil Hood, music by Walter Slaughter, Prince of Wales Theatre, 1895.
'Can you spare it?'

21. *Above.* Huntley Wright as Heliodorus in *A Greek Slave*, a musical comedy by Owen Hall, lyrics by Harry Greenbank and Adrian Ross, music by Sidney Jones, Daly's Theatre, 1898.

22. *Above right.* Marie Tempest as Maia in *A Greek Slave*.

23. *Right.* Daly's Boys, the Patricians in *A Greek Slave*.

24. *Left*. Edna May as Violet Gray in *The Belle of New York*, a musical comedy by Hugh Morton, music by Gustav Kerker, Shaftesbury Theatre, 1898. First produced in New York the previous year with little success, it was the first American musical to cross the Atlantic with its entire company and ran 697 performances.

25. *Lower left*. Frank Lawton as 'Blinkie Bill' McGuirk, and Ella Snyder as Mamie Clancy in *The Belle of New York*.

26. *Below*. Phyllis Rankin as Fifi Fricot and Harry Davenport as Harry Bronson in *The Belle of New York*.
'When we are married . . .'

27. *Right*. Marie Tempest in *San Toy*, a musical play by Edward Morton, lyrics by Harry Greenbank and Adrian Ross, music by Sidney Jones, Daly's Theatre, 1899. Marie Tempest as San Toy, disguised as a boy, wished to wear tights and short trunks, but George Edwardes insisted on knee-length shorts. The ensuing two months' quarrel, in which a pair of scissors was eventually used, resulted in the walk-out of the star and her withdrawal from the field of musical comedy.

28. *Top left*. Ada Reeve as Lady Holyrood in *Florodora*, a musical comedy by Owen Hall, lyrics by Ernest Boyd-Jones and Paul Rubens, music by Leslie Stuart, Lyric Theatre, 1899.

29. *Far left*. Sidney Barraclough as Frank Abercoed and Evie Greene as Dolores in *Florodora*.

30. *Left*. Edmund Payne and Katie Seymour in 'The Mummy Dance' from *The Messenger Boy*, a musical play by James T. Tanner and A. Murray, lyrics by Adrian Ross and Harry Greenbank, music by Ivan Caryll and Lionel Monckton, Gaiety Theatre, 1900.

31. *Above*. Gertie Millar as Cora Bellamy in *The Toreador*, a musical play by James T. Tanner and Harry Nicholls, lyrics by Adrian Ross and Percy Greenbank, music by Ivan Caryll and Lionel Monckton, Gaiety Theatre, 1901.

32. *Top right*. Connie Ediss as Mrs Malton Hoppings in *The Toreador*.

33. *Right*. Ethel Sydney, George Grossmith, Marie Studholme and Lionel Mackinder in *The Toreador*.

34. *Left*. G. P. Huntley as Lord Plantagenet, Edna May as Baroness de Tregué and Maurice Farkoa as Baron de Tregué in *Kitty Grey*, a musical comedy by J. Smyth Pigott, lyrics by Adrian Ross, music by Augustus Barratt, Howard Talbot and Lionel Monckton, Apollo Theatre, 1901.

A musical version of a comedy by the same author (from the French) which was unsuccessful the previous year at the Vaudeville Theatre.

35. *Below*. The Chinese Honeymoon, a musical play by George Dance, music by Howard Talbot, Royal Strand Theatre, 1901. The finale to Act 1.

'Bring the bridal palanquin; place the happy pair within.

To the palace haste away!'

36. *Above.* Ada Reeve as Miss Ventnor and her school girls sing 'In my Curriculum' in *The Medal and the Maid*, a musical comedy by Owen Hall, lyrics by Charles H. Taylor, George Rollit and Paul Rubens, music by Sidney Jones, Lyric Theatre, 1903.

'No middle-class ideas are known in my curriculum.'

37. *Right.* Seymour Hicks as Dicky and Ellaline Terriss as Bluebell in *Blue-Bell in Fairyland*, a musical dream play by Seymour Hicks, lyrics by Aubrey Hopwood, music by Walter Slaughter, Vaudeville Theatre, 1901. A revised version, *Blue Bell*, opened the Aldwych Theatre in 1905 and was revived on several occasions.

38. *Right*. Evie Greene as Nan in *A Country Girl*, a musical play by James T. Tanner, lyrics by Adrian Ross and Percy Greenbank, music by Lionel Monckton, Daly's Theatre, 1902.

'Try again Jo'hnnie! Try again do! . . .
But you can't get the better of a Devonshire girl!'

39. *Below*. Huntley Wright as Barry in *A Country Girl*.

'When I was a girl, a nice-minded girl,
Across the fields we'd never go in openwork stockings no, no, no!'

An additional number by Paul Rubens. It became traditional in musical comedy for the comedian at some point or other in the plot to disguise himself in female attire, a tradition which was kept alive until recent times.

40. *Top right*. Edna May as Lillian Leigh and G. P. Huntley as Sir Ormesby St Leger in *The School Girl*, a musical play by Henry Hamilton and Paul Potter, lyrics by Charles H. Taylor, music by Leslie Stuart, Prince of Wales Theatre, 1903. A strange mixture of a convent, the Stock Exchange and an artist's studio!

41. *Right*. Billie Burke as Mamie Rockfeller in *The School Girl*. She made an overnight success singing 'My Little Canoe'.

'We might canoodle, we two,
In my little canoe.'

42. *Far right*. Louis Bradfield as Harry Gordon and Ethel Irving as Winnie Harborough in *The Girl from Kay's*, a musical play by Owen Hall, lyrics by Adrian Ross and Claude Aveling, music by Cecil Cook, Apollo Theatre, 1902.

Harry steals a wedding-day kiss from the girl from Kay's, causing the matrimonial trouble and a 'semi-detached' honeymoon, cleared up only at the end of Act 2.

43. *Top left. In Dahomey.* George W. Walker as Rareback Pinkerton and Bert A. Williams as Shylock Homestead sing 'Broadway in Dahomey' in the musical comedy by Jesse A. Shipp, lyrics by Paul Lawrence Dunbar and Alex Rogers, music by Will Marion Cook, Shaftesbury Theatre, 1903.

44. *Left. In Dahomey.* Beginning the grand cake walk at the darkies' ball in Gatonville. The first all-colour musical to be produced in London.

45. *Above.* Ellaline Terriss as the Queen and chorus of canaries singing 'Good-bye Little Yellow Bird' in *The Cherry Girl*, a musical play by Seymour Hicks, lyrics by Aubrey Hopwood, music by Ivan Caryll, Vaudeville Theatre, 1903.

46. *Right.* Agnes Fraser as Elphin Haye, Walter Passmore as Jim Cheese and Henry Lytton as Dick Wargrave in *The Earl and The Girl*, a musical comedy by Seymour Hicks, lyrics by Percy Greenbank, music by Ivan Caryll, Adelphi Theatre, 1903.

47. *Left*. Gertie Millar as Lady Violet Anstruther and her Pierrots singing 'Come Along with Me', in *The Orchid*, a musical play by James T. Tanner, lyrics by Adrian Ross and Percy Greenbank, music by Ivan Caryll and Lionel Monckton, Gaiety Theatre, 1903.

48. *Below*. *The Orchid*. Lionel Mackinder, Gertie Millar, Edmund Payne, Ethel Sydney and George Grossmith in the wedding song and dance 'Our Marriage Lines'.

49. *Right*. The grand finale of *The Orchid*. The opening production of the new Gaiety Theatre in October 1903.

50. *Above.* The duel in Act I of *The Prince of Pilsen*, a musical comedy by Frank Pixley, music by Gustav Luders, Shaftesbury Theatre, 1904.
An American import, with full company, which brought Camille Clifford as Mazie Manhattan to London.

51. *Left.* C. Hayden Coffin as Harry Veneker and Sybil Arundale as Nanoya in *The Cingalee*, a musical play by James T. Tanner, lyrics by Adrian Ross and Percy Greenbank, music by Lionel Monckton, Daly's Theatre, 1904. A young English hero is again entangled with a beautiful native girl.

52. *Right.* Camille Clifford as Sylvia Gibson, the 'Gibson Girl', in *The Catch of the Season*, a musical play by Seymour Hicks and Cosmo Hamilton, lyrics by Charles H. Taylor, music by Herbert E. Haines and Evelyn Baker, Vaudeville Theatre, 1904.
The Gibson Girl hair, dress and figure, inspired by the drawings of the American artist Charles Dana Gibson, became the rage of London.

53. *Above*. The Gibson Girls, 'daughters of William Gibson', and the chorus ladies in *The Catch of the Season*. Seymour Hicks, after his break from the George Edwardes management, put on his own shows under the wing of Charles Frohman, mostly with himself and his wife, Ellaline Terriss, in the leads. He made his show girls as famous, under various names, as George Edwardes's Gaiety Girls.

54. *Left*. Seymour Hicks as the Duke of St Jermyns and Zena Dare as Angela in *The Catch of the Season*.
Hicks also followed the example of Arthur Roberts and attempted to become a leader of men's fashion. He tried to introduce knee-breeches as the *de rigeur* evening dress for the young man about town. Alas, it was not a catch of the season, although the production was a big success.

55. *Above.* The foyer of the Mascot Theatre. The opening chorus of *The Beauty of Bath*, a musical play by Seymour Hicks and Cosmo Hamilton, lyrics by Charles H. Taylor, music by Herbert E. Haines, Aldwych Theatre, 1906.

'Come to the matrimonial mart and ask for the ready maids . . .'

The young ladies (daughters of Sir Timothy and Lady Bunn) were called the Bath Buns this time and the plot was a variant on the age-old 'actor drunk to shock the heroine' theme, which has turned up many times in the theatre.

56. *Right.* Gabrielle Ray as Susan in *Lady Madcap*, a musical play by Paul Rubens and N. Newnham Davis, lyrics by Paul Rubens and Percy Greenbank, music by Paul Rubens, Prince of Wales Theatre, 1904.

The lady's maid who takes the place of her mistress, Lady Betty, the madcap who runs away from home.

57. *Above. The Dairymaids.* The gymnasium scene. A farcical musical play by A. M. Thompson and Robert Courtneidge, lyrics by Paul Rubens and Arthur Wimperis, music by Paul Rubens and Frank E. Tours, Apollo Theatre, 1906.

The last scene in Act 2 is the gymnastic department of a young ladies' seminary in which Carrie Moore 'in a symmetrion costume sings a lively ditty about the Sandow girl'.

58. *Left.* Carrie Moore sings 'The Sandow Girl' in *The Dairymaids.*

The cult of female physical fitness, spread by Eugene Sandow, was at its height at the time and made a good topical subject for a musical comedy song.

'The Gibson Girl and the Bath Bun Girl
All the world has come to know,
We like them both
And are rather loth to see either of them go,
But there's a type that can crown them all
You need not have looks nor wealth
For the girl I mean
Is the Sandow queen
The queen of all English health!'

59. *Above. The Girl behind the Counter*, a musical comedy by Leedham Bantock and Arthur Anderson, lyrics by Arthur Anderson, music by Howard Talbot, Wyndham's Theatre, 1906.
Hayden Coffin as Charlie Chetwynd, from an outpost of the Empire, leads the male chorus in 'The Land Where the Best Man Wins'.

60. *Right*. Isabel Jay as Sally in *Miss Hook of Holland*, a Dutch musical incident by Paul Rubens and Austen Hurgon, jingles and tunes by Paul Rubens, Prince of Wales Theatre, 1907.
The first of a series of musicals produced by Frank Curzon with Isabel Jay, which usually explored the world for their locales. During the long run a children's company gave matinée performances of the production, following the example of the D'Oyly Carte Children's *H.M.S. Pinafore* and *Pirates of Penzance* in earlier years.

61. *Above.* Courtice Pounds as Hugh Meredith leads the boys and girls in 'Hello! Come Along, Girls', a song from *The Belle of Mayfair*, a musical comedy by Basil Hood and Charles H. Brookfield, music by Leslie Stuart, Vaudeville Theatre, 1906.

62. *Left.* Edna May as Julia Chaldicott and Farren Soutar as the Hon. Raymond Finchley in *The Belle of Mayfair*.
Edna May left the cast soon after the opening owing to a quarrel over the prominence of Camille Clifford's Gibson Girl song. Her place was taken by the young Phyllis Dare.

63. *Above right. The Gay Gordons.* Finale, Act 1.
'Father, this is the man I love.' Barbara Deane, Ellaline Terriss, Seymour Hicks, William Lugg, Zena Dare and a highland chorus. A play with music by Seymour Hicks, lyrics by Arthur Winperis, C. H. Bovill, P. G. Wodehouse and Henry Hamilton, music by Guy Jones, Aldwych Theatre, 1907.

64. *Below*. Jean Aylwin as Minna, the Captain of the Ladies' Military College in *The Girls of Gottenberg*, a musical play by George Grossmith and L. E. Berman, lyrics by Adrian Ross and Basil Hood, music by Ivan Caryll and Lionel Monckton, Gaiety Theatre, 1907.
A musical version of the 'Koepenick' incident.

65. *Below right*. Marie Studholme as Joy Blossom in *My Darling*, a musical play by Seymour Hicks, lyrics by Charles H. Taylor, music by Herbert E. Haines, Hicks Theatre, 1907. The most ubiquitous of postcard beauties.
The theatre, built by Charles Frohman for Seymour Hicks, was renamed the Globe in 1909.

66. *Left*. Lily Elsie as Sonia and Joseph Coyne as Prince Danilo in *The Merry Widow*, a musical play by Victor Léon and Leo Stein, lyrics by Adrian Ross, music by Franz Lehár, Daly's Theatre, 1907.
The famous waltz in Act 2.

67. *Right*. Elizabeth Firth as Natalie and Robert Evett as Vicomte Camille de Jolidon sing 'Come to the Little Arbour Here', the summer-house duet in *The Merry Widow*.

68. *Below*. *The Merry Widow*, Act 3. At Maxim's. Popoff proposes to the merry widow, in the famous hat. W. H. Berry (Nisch), Irene Desmond (Sylvaine), Gordon Cleather (M. de St Brioche), Joseph Coyne (Danilo), Elizabeth Firth (Natalie), Fred Kaye (General Noviko-vich), George Graves (Baron Popoff), Nina Sevening (Olga), Lily Elsie (Sonia), V. O'Connor (Khadja) and Lennox Pawle (de Cascada).

69. *Left.* Leonard Mackay as Jackson Villiers and Evie Greene as Consuelo in *Havana*, a musical play by George Grossmith and Graham Hill, lyrics by Adrian Ross, music by Leslie Stuart, Gaiety Theatre, 1908.

'Oh, my Cuban girl
Is my pride and pearl . . .'

70. *Below.* *Havana*, a Cuban conspiracy, with W. H. Berry (Reginald Brown), Gladys Homfrey (Isabelita), Alfred Lester (Nix), Edward O'Neill (Diego de la Concha) and Robert Hale (The Hon. Frank Charteris).

71. *Above left.* Clarisse Batchelor as Marie and Maurice Farkoa as Emile Gerrard in *My Mimosa Maid*, a Riviera musical incident, written by Paul Rubens and Austen Hurgon, jingles and tunes by Paul Rubens, Prince of Wales Theatre, 1908.

'An older man has charm!'

72. *Above.* Hayden Coffin as Max Riadore and Ada Reeve as Rodanthe the witch, in *Butterflies*, a musical play by W. J. Locke, lyrics by T. H. Read, music by J. A. Robertson, Apollo Theatre, 1908.

Adapted from the same author's play *The Palace of Puck*, produced at the Haymarket Theatre the previous year.

73. *Left.* 'La Naissance du Papillon': Phyllis Monkman in *Butterflies*. This principal dancer's costume was considered quite daring in its day.

74. *Left*. Ruth Vincent as Babette and Lawrence Rea as Raymond de St Gautier in *The Belle of Brittany*, a musical play by Leedham Bantock and P. J. Barrow, lyrics by Percy Greenbank, music by Howard Talbot and Marie Horne, Queen's Theatre, 1908.
The two comedians, Walter Passmore and George Graves, were also involved in 'Daffodil Time in Brittany in the 18th Century'.

75. *Lower left*. Bertram Wallis as Alexis and Isabel Jay as Princess Marie in *King of Cadonia*, a musical play by Frederick Lonsdale, lyrics by Adrian Ross, music by Sidney Jones, Prince of Wales Theatre, 1908.
   'Thank God, at last there is a king in Cadonia.'

76. *Below*. Huntley Wright as the Duke of Alasia and Gracie Leigh as Militza in *King of Cadonia*. In a comedy song 'Disguises' Scotland comes to Cadonia.

77. *Above*. Gertie Millar as Mary Gibbs and chorus singing 'Moonstruck' in *Our Miss Gibbs*, a musical play by 'Cryptos', constructed by James T. Tanner, lyrics by Adrian Ross and Percy Greenbank, music by Ivan Caryll and Lionel Monckton, Gaiety Theatre, 1909.

'I'm such a silly when the moon comes out.'

78. *Below*. *Our Miss Gibbs*. Gladys Homfrey (the Duchess of Minster) and Denise Orme (Lady Thanet) inspect millinery at Garrod's Stores.

'Garrod's, Garrod's, all things are there! Brooches, Coaches, Tresses of hair!'

79. *Left.* Alfred Lester as Peter Doody in *The Arcadians*, a fantastic musical play by Mark Ambient and A. M. Thompson, lyrics by Arthur Wimperis, music by Lionel Monckton and Howard Talbot, Shaftesbury Theatre, 1909.

'I've gotter motter—
Always merry and bright!'

80. *Above.* Arcady comes to 'Set up the truth in England for evermore, and banish the lie', with the inevitable complications. Alfred Lester on The Deuce wins at Askwood. Nelson Keys (Bobby), Harry Welchman (Jack Meadows), Florence Smithson (Sombra), Phyllis Dare (Eileen Cavanagh) and Ada Blanche (Mrs Smith).

81. *Right.* Florence Smithson and Dan Rolyat. James Smith rejuvenated as Simplicatas is accompanied to earth by Sombra, an Arcadian maid.

'Youth and joy must have their fling
When the pipes of pan are calling . . .'

82. *Above*. A dramatic situation. The finale of Act 2, *The Dollar Princess*, a musical play by A. M. Willner and F. Grünbaum, adapted for the English stage by Basil Hood, lyrics by Adrian Ross, music by Leo Fall, Daly's Theatre, 1909.

Alice (Lily Elsie) supported by Dick (Evelyn Beerbohm) in the presence of all the guests points to Freddy Fairfax (Robert Michaelis) as the man she will marry. He rejects her autocratic decision:

> 'No, Princess, the love that's paid for, that is not what I offer you. That is not what I was made for. No, my dear, that will not do!'

83. *Left*. Evelyn Beerbohm as Dick and Gladys Cooper as Sadie Von Tromp. Starting as a Gaiety Girl, Gladys Cooper became a Daly's young lady, playing small parts before she won legitimate laurels.

84. *Above*. Seymour Hicks as Viscount Albany and Ellaline Terriss as Lucy Sheridan in *Captain Kidd*, a musical play by Seymour Hicks (from *The Dictator*, a play by Richard Harding Davis), lyrics by Adrian Ross, music by Leslie Stuart, Wyndham's Theatre, 1910.

Time off for a song and dance on board the *Bolivar*, heading for a South American revolution in San Manana.

'You could do wonders, wonders, wonders with me if you only tried . . .'

85. *Right*. Mabel Sealby as Magda and Lauri de Frece as Blatz in *The Balkan Princess*, a musical play by Frederick Lonsdale and Frank Curzon, music by Paul Rubens, Prince of Wales Theatre, 1910.

The *soubrette* and the comedian in a production which starred Isabel Jay and Bertram Wallis.

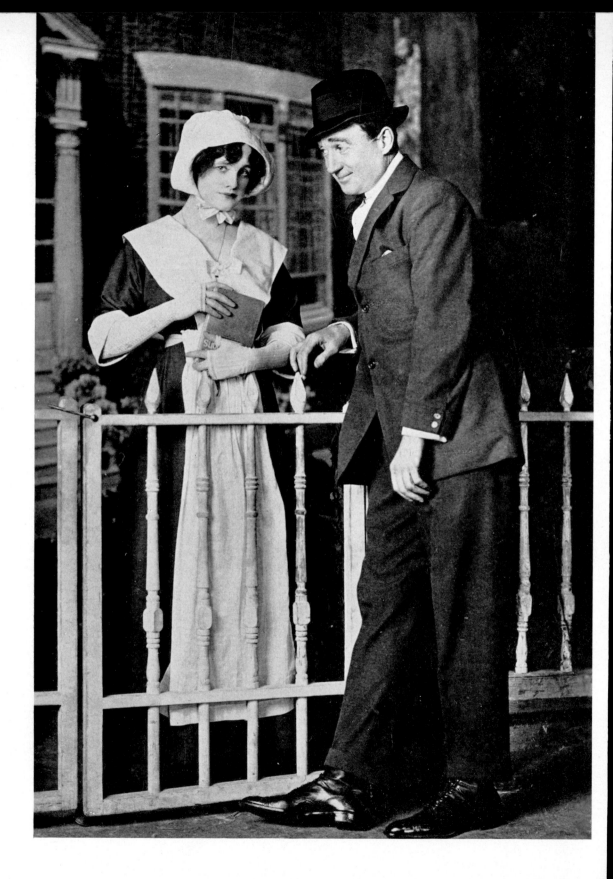

86. *Left.* Gertie Millar as Prudence and Joseph Coyne as Tony Chute in *The Quaker Girl*, a musical comedy by James T. Tanner, lyrics by Adrian Ross and Percy Greenbank, music by Lionel Monckton, Adelphi Theatre, 1910.
The Naval Attaché at the American Embassy in Paris woos the English Quaker girl.

87. *Above. Peggy*, a musical play by George Grossmith (from the French *L'Amorçage*), lyrics by Charles H. Bovill, music by Leslie Stuart, Gaiety Theatre, 1911.
London, the lounge of the New Hotel, with Phyllis Dare (Peggy Barrison), Edmund Payne (Albert Umbles), George Grossmith (Auberon Blow) and Robert Hale (the Hon. James Bendoyle, M.P., M.F.H.).

88. *Right.* Phyllis Dare as Peggy Barrison in *Peggy*. A daring bathing costume on the *plage* at Friville.
    'Go to Friville, happy Friville!
    Where the skies are always smiling.'

91. *Right*. Cicely Courtneidge as Miyo Ko San sings 'Little Japanese Mamma' in *The Mousmé*, a musical play by Alex. M. Thompson and Robert Courtneidge, lyrics by Arthur Wimperis and Percy Greenbank, music by Lionel Monckton and Howard Talbot, Shaftesbury Theatre, 1911.

    'Peeping over shoulder,
      Baby's bonny face you'll find.'
A plot in which, for once, there was no European love interest but a tremendous 'scenic' earthquake effect.

89. *Above*. Bertram Wallis as Count René of Luxembourg and Lily Elsie as Angèle Didier in *The Count of Luxembourg*, a musical play by A. M. Willner and Robert Bodanzky, adapted for the English stage by Basil Hood, lyrics by Adrian Ross and Basil Hood, music by Franz Lehár, Daly's Theatre, 1911.
A marriage of convenience is contracted under what can only be described, even in musical comedy, as extraordinary conditions:
    'Ah! She is charming I can guess!
    Though she is but a stranger,
    I should like to see her face!'

90. *Right*. Lily Elsie and Bertram Wallis in *The Count of Luxembourg*. Eventually united, they join in 'The Staircase Waltz' which went far towards rivalling its predecessor in *The Merry Widow*.
    'Stairway that leads to fairyland
    Where we may dance hand in hand!'

92. *Left.* George Grossmith as Lord Bicester, known as 'Bingo', and Phyllis Dare as Delia Dale, of the Perfume Department at Port Sunshine, in *The Sunshine Girl*, a musical play by Paul Rubens and Cecil Raleigh, lyrics by Paul Rubens and Arthur Wimperis, music by Paul Rubens, Gaiety Theatre, 1912.
With the Argentine tango beginning to supplant the waltz in popular favour, the craze is reflected in contemporary musicals.

93. *Right.* Harry Welchman as Augustin Hofer and Clara Evelyn as Princess Helen in *Princess Caprice*, a comedy with music by Alex M. Thompson (from the German), lyrics by A. Scott Craven, Harry Beswick and Percy Greenbank, music by Leo Fall, Shaftesbury Theatre, 1912.
Continental operetta, Anglicized into musical comedy, still prefers a more romantic approach to love-making between a princess and a music master.

94. *Above.* At the Jeunesse Dorée, Alec Fraser, Amy Augarde, Robert Averell, Yvonne Arnaud, Arthur Playfair and Cecily Stuckey let themselves go in *The Girl in the Taxi*, a musical play by Frederick Fenn and Arthur Wimperis, music by Jean Gilbert, Lyric Theatre, 1912.
'A merry and frolicsome scene in a Paris restaurant.'

95. *Below.* Harry Welchman as Victor Jolibeau and his six models 'Posing for Venus' in *Oh! Oh!! Delphine!!!*, a musical comedy by C. M. S. McLellan (Hugh Morton), (from the French farce *Villa Primrose*), music by Ivan Caryll, Shaftesbury Theatre, 1913.
'When I mix
The whole of the six
The Venus I get is the best one yet.'

96. *Above.* The tango at the Arts Ball in *The Girl from Utah*, a musical play by James T. Tanner and Paul Rubens, lyrics by Adrian Ross, Percy Greenbank and Paul Rubens, music by Paul Rubens and Sidney Jones, Adelphi Theatre, 1913.

'Do you tango?'
'Oh, yes, I go to all the tango teas.'

97. *Left.* Iris Hoey as Miranda Peploe in *The Pearl Girl*, a musical comedy by Basil Hood, music by Hugo Felix and Howard Talbot, Shaftesbury Theatre, 1913.
The shop girl at Palmyra Pearls (imitation) becomes the Duchess of Trent (real) in Act 3.

'You shall never go, I want no explanations, nothing but you!'

99. *Below.* Kitty Mason and George Grossmith dance the 'real' tango in *The Girl on the Film.*

98. *Above.* Emmy Whelen as Winifred ('Freddy') in *The Girl on the Film*, a musical farce by James T. Tanner, lyrics by Adrian Ross, music by Walter Kollo, Willy Bredschneider and Albert Sirmay, Gaiety Theatre, 1913.

The 'Vioscope' offices become a topical setting for the new cinema craze and Winifred, 'a tomboy', dons male attire to get an engagement as a drummer boy in a new film.

102. *Left.* Dorothy Ward as Louise ('The Film Princess') in *The Cinema Star*, a musical farcical comedy by Georg Okonkowski and Julius Freund, English version by Jack Hulbert, lyrics by Harry Graham, music by Jean Gilbert, Shaftesbury Theatre, 1914.

103. *Below.* Fay Compton as Cissie (a film actress) in *The Cinema Star*. A topical plot: a millionaire moralist and denouncer of the cinema as 'a loose entertainment' is tricked into appearing in a film himself which becomes, to his discomfort, the hit of London.

100. *Top left.* Sari Petrass as Mariposa Gilroy is rescued by Robert Michaelis as Jack Fleetwood (known as 'Slippery Jack') from the cowboys, Maurice Tosh, Edward Arundell and Frank Parfitt:
'Excuse me, boys, I met the lady first.'
The Western influence reaches the musical, in *The Marriage Market*, a musical play by Max Brody and Franz Martos, adapted by Gladys Unger, lyrics by Arthur Anderson and Adrian Ross, music by Victor Jacobi, Daly's Theatre, 1913.

101. *Left. The Marriage Market.* Finale, Act 2, on board the yacht *Maripos* anchored in San Francisco Bay. Mariposa discovers that Jack is the son of her father's old enemy, and dismisses him.

104. *Above*. Godfrey Tearle as Carlo and Phyllis Dare as Tina, in *Tina*, a musical play by Paul Rubens and Harry Graham, lyrics by Paul Rubens, Percy Greenbank and Harry Graham, music by Paul Rubens and Haydn Wood, Adelphi Theatre, 1915.

Tina, wooed incognito and by the strains of a violin, finds out the awful truth:

‘I’m not a musician at all, I’m Carlo, Duke of Borgolese, I can’t play a note of music.’

105. *Below*. *To-Night’s the Night*. James Blakeley, Leslie Henson, Peggy Kurton, Max Dearly and George Grossmith singing ‘Any Old Night’ (a Jerome Kern number) in a musical play by Fred Thompson, lyrics by Paul Rubens and Percy Greenbank, music by Paul Rubens, Gaiety Theatre, 1915.

106. *Above. Betty*, finale, Act 1. Mary Ridley (Dolly), Isabel Delorme (Chicquette), Winifred Barnes (Betty), Donald Calthrop (Gerald Earl of Beverley), Arthur Wellesley (Victor) and Daisy Burrell (David) in a musical play by Frederick Lonsdale and Gladys Unger, lyrics by Adrian Ross and Paul Rubens, music by Paul Rubens, Daly's Theatre, 1915.

'You want me for your wife?'
'You shall be Lady Beverley.'
Betty, a kitchen maid, to spite the family is asked to join the peerage, and the New Age enters the world of musical comedy.

107. *Right.* David Burnaby as Bompas, 24th Duke of Shetland, and Leslie Henson as Pony Twitchin sing 'Three Hundred and Sixty-five Days', in *Theodore and Co.*, a musical play by H. M. Harwood and George Grossmith, lyrics by Adrian Ross and Clifford Grey, music by Ivor Novello and Jerome Kern, Gaiety Theatre, 1916.

108. *Above.* The Slave Market in *Chu Chin Chow*, a musical tale of the East by Oscar Asche, music by Frederick Norton, His Majesty's Theatre, 1916.

The holder of the long-run record for a musical production until beaten by *Salad Days* twenty-eight years later.

109. *Below left.* Oscar Asche as Abu Hasan.

110. *Below right.* Lily Brayton as Zahrat-al-Kulub.

111. *Right.* Alfred Lester as Oliver Bing, Violet Loraine as Emma and George Robey as Lucifer Bing in *The Bing Boys are Here*, a picture of London life in seven panels, adapted from the French by George Grossmith and Fred Thompson, lyrics by Clifford Grey, music by Nat D. Ayre, Alhambra Theatre, 1916.

112. *Left*. Winifred Barnes as Mary, Princess of Valaria, Arthur Wontner as Charles, Prince of Talania, and José Collins as Camille Joyeuse, a queen of Bohemia, in *The Happy Day*, a musical play by Seymour Hicks, lyrics by Adrian Ross and Paul Rubens, music by Sidney Jones and Paul Rubens, Daly's Theatre, 1916.

113. *Below*. *The Boy*, the finale: Dorothy Monroe (Turner), Peter Gawthorne (Albany Pope), Nellie Taylor (Diana Fairlie), Maisie Gay (Millicent Meebles), W. H. Berry (Valentine Meebles), Heather Thatcher (Katie Muirhead), Donald Calthrop (Hughie Cavanagh), Billie Carleton (Joy Chatterton), Peter Madgewick (Tich Ridley) and Gwen Hughes (Doris Cuddley). A musical comedy by Fred Thompson, founded on *The Magistrate* by Arthur Pinero, lyrics by Adrian Ross and Percy Greenbank, music by Lionel Monckton and Howard Talbot, Adelphi Theatre, 1917.

114. *Right*. José Collins as Teresa in *The Maid of the Mountains*, a musical play by Frederick Lonsdale, lyrics by Harry Graham, music by Harold Fraser-Simpson and J. W. Tate, Daly's Theatre, 1917.

115. *Top left.* Evelyn Laye as Madeline Manners in *Going Up*, a musical comedy by James Montgomery (founded on his comedy *The Aviator*) and Otto Harbach, lyrics by Otto Harbach, music by Louis Achille Hirsch, Gaiety Theatre, 1918.

116. *Top right.* Beatrice Lillie as Jackie Sampson in *Oh! Joy*, a musical piece by Guy Bolton and P. G. Wodehouse, music by Jerome Kern, Kingsway Theatre, 1919.

117. *Left.* Leslie Henson (Bibi St Pol), Tom Walls (Col. Bolinger), George Grossmith (Max Touquet) and Yvonne Arnaud (Georgette St Pol) in *Kissing Time*, a musical play by Guy Bolton and P. G. Wodehouse (from the French), music by Ivan Caryll, Winter Garden Theatre, 1919.

118. *Above.* W. H. Berry as Valentine Hooper in *Who's Hooper?*, a musical comedy by Fred Thompson, based on Pinero's *In Chancery*, lyrics by Clifford Grey, music by Howard Talbot and Ivor Novello, Adelphi Theatre, 1919. Produced in New York as *The Girl Behind the Gun*.

119. *Left*. Edith Day as Irene O'Dare and Pat Somerset as Donald Marshall in *Irene*, a musical comedy by James Montgomery, lyrics by Joseph McCarthy, music by Harry Tierney, Empire Theatre, 1920. An American version of the Cinderella story which brought Edith Day and 'Alice Blue Gown' to London.

120. *Below*. José Collins as Sybil Renaud and the male chorus, 'The Crimson Hussars', in *Sybil*, a musical play by Max Brody and Franz Martos, English version by Harry Graham, music by Victor Jacobi, Daly's Theatre, 1921.
   'I am proud to be your Colonel, I feel I was born to command a regiment.'

121. *Right*. Dorothy Dickson as Sally of the Alley, a 'Foundling', and Leslie Henson as Constantine, Grand Duke of Czechogovinia, a waiter at the Alley Inn, in *Sally*, a musical comedy by Guy Bolton, lyrics by Arthur Grey, music by Jerome Kern, Winter Garden Theatre, 1921.

122. Courtice Pounds as Franz Schubert and Clara Butterworth as Lili Veit in *Lilac Time*, a play with music by A. M. Willner and Heinz Reichert, English version by Adrian Ross, music arranged from the melodies of Schubert by Heinrich Berté and G. H. Clutsam, Lyric Theatre, 1922.

'The Golden Song', under the lilac bough.

123. *Above*. Sydney Fairbrother (Mrs Butler), Fred Groves (Battling Butler), Jack Buchanan (Alfred Butler), Sylvia Leslie (Bertha Butler) in *Battling Butler*, a musical farce by Stanley Brightman and Austin Melford, lyrics by Douglas Furber, music by Philip Braham, New Oxford Theatre, 1922.

124. *Right*. Heather Thatcher as Lovey Toots and Leslie Henson as Odo Philpotts in *The Beauty Prize*, a musical comedy by George Grossmith and P. G. Wodehouse, music by Jerome Kern, Winter Garden Theatre, 1923.
At the 'Majestania' sports, a 'hop it' on deck.

125. *Below*. Evelyn Laye as Pompadour makes her Act 2 entrance in *Madame Pompadour*, a musical play adapted by Frederick Lonsdale and Harry Graham, lyrics by Harry Graham, music by Leo Fall, Daly's Theatre, 1923.

126. *Left.* Phyllis Dare as Mariana in *The Lady of the Rose* by Rudolph Schanzer and Ernest Welisch, a musical play adapted by Frederick Lonsdale, lyrics by Harry Graham, music by Jean Gilbert, Daly's Theatre, 1922.

127. *Right.* June as Princess Stephanie and Jack Buchanan as Anthony Prince (known as Toni) in *Toni*, a farcical musical comedy by Douglas Furber and Harry Graham, lyrics by Douglas Furber, music by Hugo Hirsch, Shaftesbury Theatre, 1924.

128. *Below.* Vera Freeman (Tutu), Maidie Andrews (succeeding Sylvia Leslie as Charlotte), Thorpe Bates (Charles, Duke of Nancy), W. H. Berry (Bouquet) and Winifred Barnes (Helene) in *The Three Graces*, a musical play by Carlo Lombordo and A. M. Willner, adapted by Ben Travers, music by Franz Lehár, Empire Theatre, 1924.

129. *Above*. Harry Welchman as Bonni and Phyllis Dare as Yvette in *The Street Singer*, a musical play by Frederick Lonsdale, lyrics by Percy Greenbank, music by Harold Fraser-Simpson, Lyric Theatre, 1924.

The leading lady makes a proposal—

    'Say this after me, "Yvette, will you marry me?" '

He does and all ends happily.

130. *Below*. Mary Leigh (Kitty), Winifred Evans (Ann), Leslie Faber (the Rev. John Head), Evelyn Laye (Betty), Arthur Margetson (Barnaby) and Jack Hobbs (Brian Ropes) in *Betty in Mayfair*, a musical play by John Hastings Turner, based on his play *The Lilies of the Field*, lyrics by Harry Graham, music by Harold Fraser-Simpson, Adelphi Theatre, 1925.

The transformation of the 'Victorian' Betty.

    'Wait a minute and you shall see me come out of my rotten pose. There Barnaby, this is me!'

131. *Above.* Lilian Davies as Katja Karina and Gregory Stroud as Prince Carl in *Katja, the Dancer*, a musical comedy by Leopold Jacobsohn and Rudolph Oesterreicher, adapted by Frederick Lonsdale and Harry Graham, lyrics by Harry Graham, music by Jean Gilbert, Gaiety Theatre, 1925.

'Oh, Katja, you're wonderful . . .'

132. *Above right.* Ivy Tresmand as Patricia and Gene Gerrard as Leander find themselves under arrest in *Katja, the Dancer*.

133. *Right.* Cicely Stevens (Helene), Cicely Debenham (Clo-Clo) and Paul England (Maxime) in *Clo-Clo*, a farcical musical comedy by Douglas Furber and Harry Graham, music by Franz Lehár, Shaftesbury Theatre, 1925.

'Let me stay with you night and day, 'twould be bliss divine.'

Sung to a violin obbligato!

134. *Left.* Adele Astaire as Suzanne Hayden and Fred Astaire as Teddy Lawrence in *Stop Flirting*, a musical farce by Frederick Jackson, music by William Daly and Paul Lannin, Shaftesbury Theatre, 1923.

The Astaires on their first visit to London, sing 'The Whichness of the Whatness' and dance the Oom-pa trot.

'Whenever this little satire upon the manners and customs of the modern house faintly shows any signs of slowing down, these two brilliant young dancers come on and set it spinning merrily again.'

135. *Right.* Vera Lennox as Bonnie Reeves and Claude Hulbert as Billy in *Tell Me More*, a musical comedy by Fred Thompson and William K. Wells, lyrics by B. G. De Syla, Desmond Carter and Ira Gershwin, music by George Gershwin, Winter Garden Theatre, 1925.

The comedy team sing 'How Can I Win You Now?' and indulge in some eccentric dancing.

In this production Leslie Henson and Heather Thatcher who played the leads also indulged in 'numerous and fantastically applauded dances, most of them noted rather for agility and acrobatic ingenuity than for grace and elegance.'

136. *Above.* Mira Nirska as Wanda heads the chorus in the Totem Dance, 'Totem Tom-Tom', in *Rose Marie*, a musical play, 'a romance of the Canadian Rockies', by Otto Harbach and Oscar Hammerstein II, music by Rudolf Friml and Herbert Stothart, Theatre Royal, Drury Lane, 1925.

'Barbaric head-dresses and picturesque Redskin garb are worn by the members of the immense chorus of Totem Pole Girls, who sway and fall like countless ears of corn in a wind, and move with such precision and splendid unity that it seems incredible that they should be different individuals.'

Number Five from the left in the front row is Anna Neagle (then Marjorie Robertson).

137. *Right.* Edith Day as Rose Marie in the first of the spectacular American musicals at Drury Lane, which were to occupy the theatre for the next ten years. It was revived there in 1929.

138. *Left*. Binnie Hale as Nanette and Seymour Beard as Tom Trainor in *No, No, Nanette*, a musical comedy by Frank Mandel, Otto Harbach and Irving Caesar, adapted from the play *His Lady Friends* by Emile Nyitray and Frank Mandel (based on the novel by May Edgington), music by Vincent Youmans, Palace Theatre, 1925.

'Tea for two and two for tea,
Me for you and you for me . . .'

139. *Below*. Florence Bayfield as Winnie, Joan Barry as Betty, Vera Pearce as Flora, with Joseph Coyne as Jimmy Smith and George Grossmith as Billy Early in *No, No, Nanette*.

'I want to be happy
But I can't be happy
Till I make you happy too.'

140. *Above.* Irene Browne in *No, No, Nanette.* Lucille with the bachelors singing the blues.

　'Where has my hubby gone?'—

　'Throw away his photograph, until you find a better half . . .'

Because it has often been cut in revivals this is one of the lesser known numbers.

141. *Below.* Peggy O'Neil as Mary in *Mercenary Mary*, a musical comedy by Frederick Jackson, lyrics by Irving Caesar, music by William B. Friedlander and Con Conrad, London Hippodrome, 1925.

　'All the men are so mercenary, Mary, That you've got to be mercenary too.'

142. *Above*. William Kent as J. Watterson Watkins sings the title song in *Lady, be Good!*, a musical comedy by Guy Bolton and Fred Thompson, lyrics by Ira Gershwin, music by George Gershwin, Empire Theatre, 1926.

143. *Below*. George Grossmith as Christian II of Sylvania, Winnie Melville as Princess Elaine of Novia, John Clarke as Captain Torelli (of the battle-cruiser *Fire-eater*) and Ernest Graham as Attorney General in *Princess Charming*, a romance with music by Franz Martos, adapted by Arthur Wimperis and Lauri Wylie, lyrics by Arthur Wimperis, music by Albert Szirmai, Palace Theatre, 1926.
The Princess refuses to obey the King and sign the papers divorcing her from Captain Torelli.

144. *Right*. Gertrude Lawrence as Kay in *Oh, Kay!*, a musical comedy by Guy Bolton and P. G. Wodehouse, lyrics by Ira Gershwin, music by George Gershwin, His Majesty's Theatre, 1927. The first English star to create a part on Broadway before bringing the piece to London.

145. *Left.* Harry Welchman as Pierre Birabeau (the Red Shadow) and Edith Day as Margot Bonvalet in *The Desert Song*, a musical play by Oscar Hammerstein II, Otto Harbach and Frank Mandel, music by Sigmund Romberg, Theatre Royal, Drury Lane, 1927.

'Come a step nearer and I fire.'
'There is your pistol, and here is my heart.'

146. *Below.* Nancie Lovat (Marcia Manners), Jack Buchanan (Jim Demming), Binnie Hale ('Sunny' Peters), Jack Hobbs (Tom Warren) and Elsie Randolph ('Weenie' Winters) in *Sunny*, a musical comedy by Otto Harbach and Oscar Hammerstein II, music by Jerome Kern, London Hippodrome, 1926.

147. *Above*. Derek Oldham (François Villon), H. A. Saintsbury (Louis XI) and Winnie Melville (Katherine de Vaucelles) in *The Vagabond King*, a romantic musical play by W. H. Post and Brian Hooker, based on Justin Huntley Mc-Carthy's *If I Were King*, music by Rudolf Friml, Winter Garden Theatre, 1927.
All ends happily:

> 'Sire, your sentence must today be reversed,
> for I claim to marry this gentleman.'

148. *Below*. Emma Haig as Jennie with the girls performs 'Step on the Blues' in *The Girl Friend*, a musical comedy based on *Kitty's Kisses* by Philip Bartholomae and Otto Harbach, adapted for the London stage by R. P. Weston and Bert Lee, lyrics by Lorenz Hart, Con Conrad and Gus Kahn, music by Richard Rodgers, Palace Theatre, 1927.

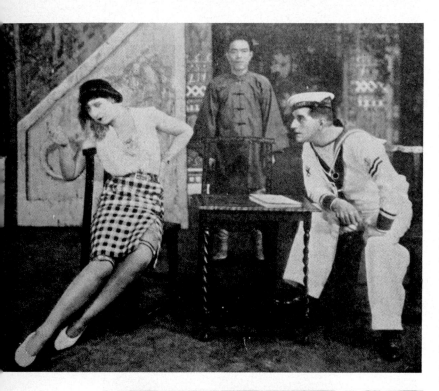

149. *Left.* Ellen Pollock as Rita and Stanley Holloway as Bill Smith in *Hit the Deck*, a musical comedy by Herbert Fields, based on the play *Shore Leave* by Hubert Osborne, lyrics by Leo Rohn and Clifford Grey, Anglicized and adapted for the English stage by R. P. Weston and Bert Lee, music by Vincent Youmans, London Hippodrome, 1927.

150. *Lower left.* Jack Buchanan as Bill Barrow in *That's a Good Girl*, a musical comedy by Douglas Furber, lyrics by Douglas Furber, Ira Gershwin and Desmond Carter, music by Philip Charig and Joseph Meyer, London Hippodrome, 1928.

151. *Below.* Cyril Ritchard as the Hon. Peter Malden and Madge Elliott as Pamela Stuart in *So This is Love*, a musical play by Stanley Lupino and Arthur Rigby, lyrics by Desmond Carter, music by Hal Brody, Winter Garden Theatre, 1928.

152. *Above*. Laddie Cliff as Hap J. Haggard, Gilly Flower as Billie St John and Dudley Rolph as Guy Steeple, with the assistance of the entire chorus, sing and dance 'Hop on Your Toes' in *So This is Love*.

153. *Below*. Viola Compton (Parthy Ann Hawks), Edith Day (Magnolia), Dorothy Lena (Ellie), Marie Burke (Julie), Colin Clive (Steve), Cedric Hardwicke (Captain Andy), Jack Martin (Windy), Percy Parsons (Vallon), Alberta Hunter (Queenie) and Paul Robeson (Joe) in *Show Boat*, a musical play by Oscar Hammerstein II, music by Jerome Kern, adapted from the novel by Edna Ferber, Theatre Royal, Drury Lane, 1928.

154. *Left.* Evelyn Laye as Marianne in *The New Moon*, a romantic musical play by Oscar Hammerstein II, Frank Mandel and Laurence Schwab, music by Sigmund Romberg, Theatre Royal, Drury Lane, 1929.

'And while I'm waiting here
This heart of mine is singing,
Lover, come back to me.'

155. *Right.* Peggy Wood as Sarah Millick and George Metaxa as Carl Linden in *Bitter-Sweet*, book, lyrics and music by Noël Coward, His Majesty's Theatre, 1929.

'I'll see you again,
Whenever Spring breaks through again . . .'

156. *Left.* Peggy Wood as Sarah, now Sari Linden, and Ivy St Helier as Manon (La Crevette) in *Bitter-Sweet*.

'All is well, my dear—I don't love him any more, really, at least I don't think I do, and anyhow you have no reason to be jealous, nothing to be afraid of. Look at me, and then look in the glass.'

Carl became the first leading man to be killed before the last act.

157. *Above.* Fred Astaire as Jimmy Reeve in *Funny Face* by Frederick Thompson and Paul Gerard Smith, lyrics by Ira Gershwin, music by George Gershwin, Princes Theatre, 1928.

'High hat, you've got to treat them, high hat, Don't let them know that you care . . .'

158. *Below.* Fred Astaire as Jimmy Reeve and Adele Astaire as Frankie Wynne in *Funny Face.*

'I love your funny face, your sunny, funny face . . .'

159. *Right.* Laddie Cliff as Rolly Ryder and Stanley Lupino as Jerry Walker in *Love Lies*, a musical play by Stanley Lupino and Arthur Rigby, lyrics by Desmond Carter, music by Hal Brody, Gaiety Theatre, 1929.

The drinking scene, a timeless comedy routine.

160. *Below*. Sophie Tucker as Georgia Madison and Jack Hulbert as Bobby Hilary sing 'Going Home' in *Follow a Star*, by Douglas Furber and Dion Titheradge, lyrics by Douglas Furber, music by Vivian Ellis, Winter Garden Theatre, 1930.
A rare appearance in Musical Comedy of the great Cabaret and Vaudeville entertainer.

161. *Above*. Bobby Howes as Jim and Binnie Hale as Jill Kemp in *Mr Cinders*, a musical comedy by Clifford Grey and Greatrex Newman, music by Vivian Ellis and Richard Myers, Adelphi Theatre, 1929.
The Cinderella story in reverse. The millionaire's daughter masquerading as a maid meets 'Mr Cinders' whom she sends to the ball, having warned him:
'I'm a one-man girl who's looking for a one-girl man.'

162. *Top right*. Clarice Hardwicke as Betty Boyd leads the male chorus in 'The Lass who Loves a Sailor' in *Heads Up!*, a musical comedy by John McGowan and Paul Gerard Smith, adapted for the English stage by Lauri Wylie, lyrics by Lorenz Hart, music by Richard Rodgers, Palace Theatre, 1930.

163. *Lower right*. Rita Page as Dolly and the girls perform 'The Kinkajou' in *Rio Rita*, a romantic musical comedy by Guy Bolton and Fred Thompson, lyrics by Joseph McCarthy, music by Harry Tierney, Prince Edward Theatre, 1930.
This production opened the new theatre in Soho now called the London Casino.

164. *Left.* Sonnie Hale as Tommy Thompson and Jessie Matthews as Harriet Green sing 'Dancing on the Ceiling' in *Ever Green*, a musical show by Benn Levy, lyrics by Lorenz Hart, music by Richard Rodgers, Adelphi Theatre, 1930.

'How I love my ceiling more
Now it is my dancing floor . . .'

One of C. B. Cochran's most lavish productions which opened the rebuilt Adelphi Theatre.

165. *Right.* Carl Brisson as Harry and Dorothy Dickson as Liane sing 'I'll Believe in Love', in *Wonder Bar*, a musical play by Geza Herczeg and Karl Farkas, arranged for the English stage by Rowland Leigh, music by Robert Katscher, Savoy Theatre, 1930.

The stage and auditorium were united by Basil Ionides in a cabaret setting which brought a new dimension to the musical stage.

166. *Right.* Frederick Leister as the Emperor, Lea Seidl as Josepha Voglhuber and Clifford Mollison as Leopold in *White Horse Inn*, a spectacular musical play, adapted from the comedy *Blumenthal und Kadelburg* by Hans Muller, English version by Harry Graham, music by Ralph Benatsky and Robert Stolz, Coliseum, 1931.
The Emperor is greeted by Josepha on his arrival to stay at the White Horse Inn for the shooting season.
London's first taste of a German realistic spectacular production which used all three revolving stages of the theatre and spilt over into the auditorium.

167. *Left.* Stanley Lupino as Eddy Marston, Sonnie Hale as Pop Curry, Margery Wyn as Helen and Jessie Matthews as Paula Bond sing 'Spring' in *Hold My Hand*, a musical comedy by Stanley Lupino, lyrics by Desmond Carter, music by Noel Gay, Gaiety Theatre, 1931.

168. *Above.* The grand finale in *Waltzes from Vienna*, a love story of music by A. M. Willner, Heinz Reichert and Ernst Marischka, arranged for the English stage by Desmond Carter and Caswell Garth, music by Johann Strauss (father and son), arranged by G. H. Clutsam, Herbert Griffiths, E. W. Korngold and Julius Bittner, Alhambra Theatre, 1931.
Strauss snr. acclaims his son's 'The Blue Danube'.

169. *Below.* Richard Tauber as Prince Sou Chong in *The Land of Smiles*, a musical play by Ludwig Herzer and Fritz Löhner, from the original by Victor Léon, adapted for the English stage by Harry Graham, music by Franz Lehár, Theatre Royal, Drury Lane, 1931.

170. *Top right. Casanova.* The carnival scene. A musical play of adventure and love, adapted by Hans Müller (after Schanzer and Welisch), arranged for the English stage by Harry Graham, music by Johann Strauss (arranged by Ralph Benatsky), Coliseum, 1932.

171. *Lower right.* Peter Haddon (Dick), Bobby Howes (Bobbie), Jean Adrienne (Gwen), Alfred Drayton (Ralston) and Jack Lambert (Maclean) in *Tell Her the Truth*, a play with tunes, based on the play *Nothing but the Truth* by James Montgomery and the book of the same name by Frederick S. Isham, adaptation and lyrics by R. P. Weston and Bert Lee, music by Jack Waller and Joseph Tunbridge, Saville Theatre, 1932.

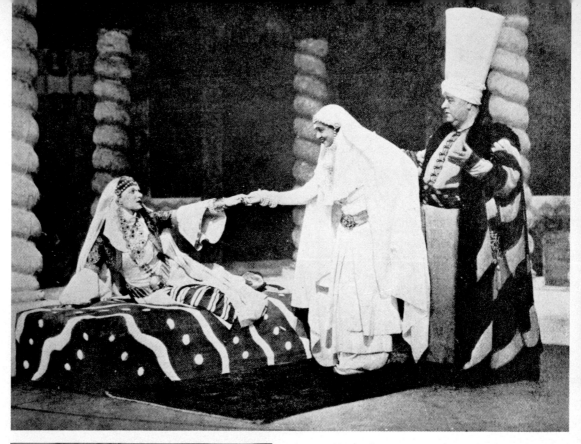

172. *Above*. Gertrude Lawrence as Evangeline, Elizabeth Welch as Haidee Robinson and Bruce Winston as Ali: 'A Harem in Turkey' in *Nymph Errant*, a play with music by Romney Brent, adapted from a novel by James Laver, lyrics and music by Cole Porter, Adelphi Theatre, 1933.

173. *Left*. Fred Astaire as Guy Holden and Claire Luce as Mimi in *Gay Divorce*, an intimate musical comedy by Dwight Taylor, music and lyrics by Cole Porter, Palace Theatre, 1933.

'Night and day,
You are the one . . .'

174. *Above.* Arthur Riscoe as Jack Crawford and Frances Day as Jill Sonning in *Jill, Darling!*, a musical comedy by Marriott Edgar and Desmond Carter, music by Vivian Ellis, Saville Theatre, 1934.

'Let's lay our heads together . . .'

175. *Above right.* Elsie Randolph as Betty Trotter and Jack Buchanan as Dick Whittington in *Mr Whittington*, a musical show by Clifford Grey, Greatrex Newman and Douglas Furber, music by John W. Green, Jack Waller and Joseph Tunbridge, London Hippodrome, 1934.

'Who do you think you are?'

176. *Right.* Louis Hayward as the Marquis of Sheere, Noël Coward as Paul, Duc de Chaucigny-Varennes, and Yvonne Printemps as Melanie in *Conversation Piece*, a romantic comedy with music by Noël Coward, His Majesty's Theatre, 1934.

177. *Above left*. Ivor Novello as Anthony Allen has a gipsy wedding in *Glamorous Night*, a musical play devised, written and composed by Ivor Novello, lyrics by Christopher Hassell, Theatre Royal, Drury Lane, 1935.

178. *Above*. Mary Ellis as Militza Hajos, on board the S.S. *Silver Star* in *Glamorous Night*.

179. *Left*. Bobby Howes as Tommy Deacon, Wylie Watson as Mr Clutterbuck and Vera Pearce as Miss Trundle in *Please Teacher!*, a musical comedy by K. R. G. Browne, R. P. Weston and Bert Lee, lyrics by R. P. Weston and Bert Lee, music by Jack Waller and Joseph Tunbridge, London Hippodrome, 1935.
The sleep-walking scene in the dormitory of the girls' school.

180. *Right.* Vera Zorina, Sergieff and Jack Whiting in 'Slaughter on Tenth Avenue', the ballet in *On Your Toes*, a musical comedy by Richard Rodgers, Lorenz Hart and George Abbott, lyrics by Lorenz Hart, music by Richard Rodgers, Palace Theatre, 1937.
Modern ballet, by George Balanchine, enters the world of musical comedy for the first time.

181. *Below.* Ivor Novello as Michae Alderney and Dorothy Dickson as Penelope Lee in *Careless Rapture*, a musical play devised, written and composed by Ivor Novello, lyrics by Christopher Hassell, Theatre Royal, Drury Lane, 1936.
The Chinese dream ballet (by Anthony Tudor) in which the hero and heroine re-live the legend of the Temple of Nichaow.

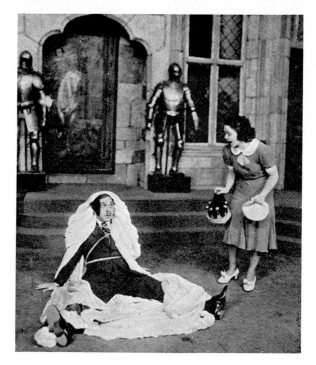

182. *Above.* Gavin Gordon (Nikolas), Richard Caldicot (Pantages), Fred Emney (Pallas Pollicapillos), Leslie Henson (Alexandros Saggapopolous), Muriel White (Juno), Richard Hearne (Thomasso Mogolini), Mary Lawson (Pomono Polliccapillos) and Roy Royston (Leander) in *Going Greek*, a musical show by Guy Bolton, Fred Thompson and Douglas Furber, lyrics and music by Lerner, Goodhart and Hoffman, Gaiety Theatre, 1937.

Musical comedy still flourishing in the final years of the Gaiety Theatre.

183. *Left.* Lupino Lane as Bill Snibson and Teddie St Denis as Sally in *Me and My Girl*, a musical comedy by L. Arthur Rose and Douglas Furber, music by Noel Gay, Victoria Palace, 1937.

'My lords, I rise to my feet.'

184. *Above.* Ian Maclean (Ricky), Bobby Howes (Tommy), Cicely Courtneidge (Sally) and David Burns (Bennie) in *Hide and Seek*, a musical play by Guy Bolton, Fred Thompson and Douglas Furber, lyrics and music by Vivian Ellis, Lerner, Goodhart and Hoffman, London Hippodrome, 1937. The comedians in the usual tight corner.

185. *Right.* Wylie Watson as Chester Binney, Bertha Belmore as Mrs Simmons and Sydney Howard as Mr Simmons in *Oh! You Letty*, a musical comedy by Geoffrey Kerr, Bert Lee and Clifford Grey, founded on the play *The Whole Town's Talking* by John Emerson and Anita Loos, music by Paul Sharon, Palace Theatre, 1937.

186. *Left*. Kenneth Carten as Lord Camp, Ross Landon as Lord Borrowmere, John Gatrell as Lord Sickert and Hugh French as Lord Elderley in *Operette*, a musical play written and composed by Noël Coward, His Majesty's Theatre, 1938.

'The Stately Homes of England
How beautiful they stand,
To prove the upper classes
Have still the upper hand . . .'

187. *Right*. Cicely Courtneidge as Kay Porter and Jack Hulbert as Jack Millet in *Under Your Hat*, a musical comedy by Archie Menzies, Arthur Macrae and Jack Hulbert, lyrics and music by Vivian Ellis, Palace Theatre, 1938.

Jack and Kay disguised as the two mechanics, having gained possession of a carburettor in spite of foreign spies, at last fly back to England to a happy ending.

188. *Above.* Ivor Novello as Rudi Kleber and Mary Ellis as Maria Ziegler in *The Dancing Years*, a musical play devised, written and composed by Ivor Novello, lyrics by Christopher Hassall, Theatre Royal, Drury Lane, 1939.
Maria buys the 'Waltz of my heart':
    'Here, Mr Rudi Kleber, is your thousand kronen.'

189. *Right.* Patricia Burke as 'Gay' Girard in *The Lisbon Story*, a musical play by Harold Purcell, music by Harry Parr-Davies, London Hippodrome, 1943.
'A battle of wits, with love and British agents intervening, between von Schriner of the Berlin Cultural Department and the French actress "Gay" Girard. She returns to Paris from Lisbon but only to help a French scientist escape from internment. His daughter is given a small part in the new ballet at the Mogador Theatre. Von Schriner suspects Gay's motives, but hopes to blackmail her into living with him. While the escape is on, Gay impersonates the daughter in the ballet and rouses the audience in a patriotic speech. The Marseillaise, revolver shots and British bombs ring down the curtain'. On the death of the leading lady—for the first time!

190. *Above*. Claude Hulbert as Vivian Budd, Bebe Daniels as Hattie Maloney and Richard Hearne as Loopy Smith in *Panama Hattie*, a musical play by Herbert Fields and B. G. De Sylva, songs by Cole Porter, Piccadilly Theatre, 1943.
Hattie, estranged from her boy friend, drowns her sorrows in the bar of The Tropical Shore.

191. *Left*. Cicely Courtneidge as Jo Fox and Thorley Walters as Tim Garret in *Under the Counter*, a comedy with music by Arthur Macrae, lyrics by Harold Purcell, music by Manning Sherwin, Phoenix Theatre, 1945.
    'A memory of old Japan . . .'

192. *Right*. Ivor Novello as Sir Graham Rodney in *Perchance to Dream*, a musical romance, devised, written and composed by Ivor Novello, London Hippodrome, 1945.

193. *Left.* Lizbeth Webb as Lucy Veracity Willow in *Bless the Bride*, a musical show by A. P. Herbert, music by Vivian Ellis, Adelphi Theatre, 1947.

'I sometimes wish my heart could speak and say—what my poor lips can never tell.'

194. *Below.* Betty Jane Watson as Laurey and Howard Keel as Curly in *Oklahoma!*, a musical play by Oscar Hammerstein II, based on the play *Green Grow the Lilacs* by Lynn Riggs, music by Richard Rodgers, Theatre Royal, Drury Lane, 1947. Laurey and Curly leaving in the Surrey with the fringe on top!

195. *Above.* Dolores Gray as Annie Oakley and Bill Johnson as Frank Butler in *Annie Get Your Gun*, by Herbert and Dorothy Fields, lyrics and music by Irving Berlin, Coliseum, 1947.

'Anything you can do, I can do better . . .'

196. *Above right.* Aud Johansen as Caprice and Fred Emney as Fred Piper in *Blue for a Boy, or What Shall We Do with the Body?*, a musical romp by Austin Melford based on his play *It's a Boy* (from the German of Franz Arnold and Ernest Bach), lyrics by Harold Purcell, music by Harry Parr-Davics, His Majesty's Theatre, 1950.

197. *Below.* Robert Andrews (Vanescu), Zena Dare (Queen Elana of Murania), Olive Gilbert (Countess Vera Lemainken), Phyllis Dare (Marta Karillos), Ivor Novello (Nikki) and Vanessa Lee (Princess Cristiane) in *King's Rhapsody*, a musical romance devised, written and composed by Ivor Novello, lyrics by Christopher Hassall, Palace Theatre, 1949.

Mistress and wife face each other at a court ball.

198. *Above.* Graham Payn as Harry Hornby, Pat Kirkwood as Pinkie Leroy and Elwyn Brook-Jones as Joseph Snyder in *Ace of Clubs*, a musical play by Noël Coward, Cambridge Theatre, 1950. The Navy gets tough in a night club.

199. *Above right.* Iva Withers as Julie Jordan and Stephen Douglass as Billy Bigelow in *Carousel*, a musical play by Oscar Hammerstein II, based on Ferenc Molnar's *Liliom*, as adapted by Benjamin F. Glazer, music by Richard Rodgers, Theatre Royal, Drury Lane, 1950.

The leading man again dies at the end of the first half but returns as a ghost in time for the final curtain.

200. *Below.* Ray Walston as Luther Billis and Mary Martin as Ensign Nellie Forbush in *South Pacific*, a musical play by Oscar Hammerstein II and Joshua Logan, adapted from *Tales of the South Pacific* by James A. Michener, lyrics by Oscar Hammerstein II, music by Richard Rodgers, Theatre Royal, Drury Lane, 1951.

201. *Above.* Patricia Morison as Lilli Vanessi, Bill Johnson as Fred Graham, Julie Wilson as Lois Lane and Walter Long as Bill Calhoun in *Kiss Me, Kate*, a musical comedy by Sam and Bella Spewack, lyrics and music by Cole Porter, Coliseum, 1951.

The actors as Katherine, Petruchio, Bianca and Lucentio in a production of *The Taming of the Shrew*, sing 'We Open in Venice', in the backstage story of an American theatrical company on tour.

202. *Right.* Jean Carson as Jerusha Abbott in *Love from Judy*, a musical play by Eric Maschwitz, based on Jean Webster's *Daddy Long Legs*, lyrics by Hugh Martin and Jack Gray, music by Hugh Martin, Saville Theatre, 1952.

Judy cheers up the girls after their disappointment at missing the *Mardi Gras* by singing 'I'll never dream when I'm asleep'.

203. *Left.* Herbert Lom as the King and Valerie Hobson as Anna Leonowens in *The King and I*, a musical play by Oscar Hammerstein II, based on *Anna and the King of Siam* by Margaret Landon, music by Richard Rodgers, Theatre Royal, Drury Lane, 1953.

'Shall we dance?'

204. *Below left.* Ann Rogers as Polly Browne and Anthony Hayes as Tony in *The Boy Friend*, a new musical comedy of the 1920s by Sandy Wilson, Players' Theatre, 1953. First produced in a short two-act version in April, it was enlarged and produced again at the Players' Theatre in October, transferring to Wyndham's Theatre in 1954.

205. *Below.* Maria Charles (Dulcie), James Thompson (Marcel), Fred Stone (Percival Browne), Joan Sterndale Bennett (Mme Dubonnet), John Rutland (Lord Brockhurst), Anne Wakefield (Maisie) and Larry Drew (Bobbie Van Husen) in *The Boy Friend*, Players' Theatre, 1953.

It ran for 2,084 performances and is now sixth in the long run list. A revival at the Comedy Theatre in 1967 ran for nearly a year.

206. *Above*. Pat Heywood, Alan Dobie, Dorothy Reynolds, Michael Meacham, Norman
Rossington, Yvonne Coulette, Bob Harris,
Eleanor Drew, John Warner, Christine Finn
and Basil Henson in *Salad Days*, a musical
play by Dorothy Reynolds and Julian Slade,
music by Julian Slade, Theatre Royal,
Bristol, 1954.
The finale to Act 1 of the original production
which transferred, with changes of cast, to the
Vaudeville Theatre and beat the existing
long-run record for a musical held by *Chu
Chin Chow*.

207. *Right*. Harold Lang as Joey and Carol
Bruce as Vera Simpson in *Pal Joey*, a musical
play by John O'Hara, lyrics by Lorenz Hart,
music by Richard Rodgers, Princes Theatre,
1954.
Joey, the first musical 'anti-hero' pretends to
show his indifference for Vera.

208. *Top left.* Donald Eccles (Omar), Peter Croft (Caliph), Doretta Morrow (Marsinah), Alfred Drake (Hajj) and Joan Diener (Lalume) in *Kismet*, a musical Arabian Night, by Charles Lederer and Luther Davis, founded on the play by Edward Knoblock, lyrics and music by Robert Wright and George Forrest, adapted from themes of Borodin, Stoll Theatre, 1955.

209. *Lower left.* Linda Gray (Mrs Eynsford-Hill), Alan Dudley (Lord Boxington), Elaine Garreau (Lady Boxington), Robert Coote (Colonel Pickering), Rex Harrison (Henry Higgins), Julie Andrews (Eliza Doolittle), Leonard Weir (Freddy Eynsford-Hill) and Zena Dare (Mrs Higgins) in *My Fair Lady*, a musical by Alan Jay Lerner, adapted from Bernard Shaw's play *Pygmalion*, music by Frederick Loewe, Theatre Royal, Drury Lane, 1958.
The Ascot scene.

210. *Above.* George Chakiris (Rigg), Ken Le Roy (Bernardo) and Don McKay (Tony) in *West Side Story*, a musical by Arthur Laurents, based on a conception by Jerome Robbins, lyrics by Stephen Sondheim, music by Leonard Bernstein, Her Majesty's Theatre, 1958.
Tony, climbing over the fence, tries to stop the rumble between Rigg of the Jets and Bernardo of the Sharks in a modern American version of the Romeo and Juliet story.

211. *Below.* Roderick Jones (Sir Victor Vatt), Fenella Fielding (Lady Parvulade Panzoust), Doris Hare (Grannie Tooke), Patsy Rowlands (Thetis Tooke) and Peter Gilmore (David Tooke) in *Valmouth*, a musical by Sandy Wilson, adapted from the novel by Ronald Firbank, Lyric Theatre, Hammersmith, 1958.
The production eventually transferred to the Saville Theatre.

212. *Above*. Sally Adams (A Wench), Frederick Jaeger (Ramble), Stephanie Voss (Hilaret), Richard Wordsworth (Justice Squeezum), Hy Hazell (Mrs Squeezum), Terence Cooper (Constant), Madeleine Newbury (Cloris) in *Lock Up Your Daughters*, a musical by Bernard Miles, adapted from Henry Fielding's *Rape Upon Rape*, lyrics by Lionel Bart, music by Laurie Johnson, Mermaid Theatre, 1959.

213. *Left*. Georgia Brown as Nancy, Ron Moody as Fagin, Keith Hampshire as Oliver Twist and Diane Gray as Bet in *Oliver*, a musical by Lionel Bart, freely adapted from Charles Dickens's *Oliver Twist*, New Theatre, 1960.

'It's a fine life.'
The holder of the longest-run record with 2,618 performances.

214. *Above.* Jean Bayless as Maria Rainer in *The Sound of Music*, a musical play by Howard Lindsay and Russel Crouse, suggested by *The Trapp Family Singers* by Maria Augusta Trapp, lyrics by Oscar Hammerstein II, music by Richard Rodgers, Palace Theatre, 1961.

Maria, the governess, with the Von Trapp children, teaching them to sing 'Do-Re-Me'. A close contender and runner-up for the long-run record with 2,386 performances.

215. *Below left.* Elaine Stritch as Mimi Paragon in *Sail Away*, a musical, with book, music and lyrics by Noël Coward, Savoy Theatre, 1962.

216. *Below right.* Miriam Karlin as Lily Smith and Glynn Edwards as Frederick Cochran in *Fings Ain't Wot They Used T'Be*, a musical by Frank Norman, lyrics and music by Lionel Bart, Garrick Theatre, 1960.

Originally produced at the Theatre Royal, Stratford at the beginning of 1959, it was revised and revived at Stratford at the end of the same year and later transferred to the Garrick Theatre.

217. *Left.* Dora Bryan as Lorelei Lee in *Gentlemen Prefer Blondes*, a musical by Joseph Fields and Anita Loos, adapted from the novel by Anita Loos, lyrics by Leo Robin, music by Jule Styne, Princes Theatre, 1962.

'Diamonds are a girl's best friend.'

218. *Above left.* Tommy Steele as Arthur Kipps and Marti Webb as Ann in *Half A Sixpence*, a musical by Beverley Cross, based on H. G. Wells's *Kipps*, lyrics and music by David Heneker, Cambridge Theatre, 1963.
Kipps and Ann, in love, exchange as tokens halves of a sixpence and sing the title song.

219. *Above right.* Harry Secombe as Mr Pickwick and Jessie Evans as Mrs Bardell in *Pickwick*, a musical by Wolf Mankowitz, based on the novel by Charles Dickens, lyrics by Leslie Bricusse, music by Cyril Ornadel, Saville Theatre, 1963.

220. *Below.* Elizabeth Larner as Guenevere, Laurence Harvey as Arthur and Barry Kent as Lancelot in *Camelot*, a musical by Alan Jay Lerner, based on *The Once and Future King*, by T. H. White, music by Frederick Loewe, Theatre Royal, Drury Lane, 1964.
Guenevere meets Lancelot the young knight from France.

221. *Left.* June Bronhill as Elizabeth Moulton-Barrett with Dewcroft Pandora as Flush in *Robert and Elizabeth*, a musical by Ronald Millar, from an original idea by Fred G. Moritt, based on the play *The Barretts of Wimpole Street*, by Rudolf Besier, music by Ron Grainer, Lyric Theatre, 1964.

222. *Above left.* Mary Martin as Mrs Dolly Gallagher Levi in *Hello Dolly!* by Michael Stewart, based on Thornton Wilder's play *The Matchmaker*, lyrics and music by Jerry Herman, Theatre Royal, Drury Lane, 1965.
Dolly, at the Harmonia Gardens Restaurant, singing the title song.

223. *Above right.* Danny La Rue as Danny Rhodes in *Come Spy With Me*, a musical comedy—book, lyrics and music by Bryan Blackburn, Whitehall Theatre, 1966.
What can happen in a musical-comedy M.I.5.

224. *Right.* Joe Brown as Joe and Anna Neagle as Lady Hadwell in *Charlie Girl*, a musical by Hugh and Margaret Williams and Ray Cooney on a story by Ross Taylor, lyrics by John Taylor and David Heneker, music by David Heneker, Adelphi Theatre, 1965.
'You never know what you can do until you try.'

225. *Left.* Topol as Tevye and Miriam Karlin as Golda in *Fiddler on the Roof*, a musical by Joseph Stein, based on Sholem Aleichem's stories, lyrics by Sheldon Harnick, music by Jerry Bock, Her Majesty's Theatre, 1967.
  'Do you love me?'
Later in the long run Topol and Miriam Karlin were succeeded by Alfie Bass and Avis Bunnage.

226. *Below left.* Juliet Prowse as Charity in *Sweet Charity*, a musical by Neil Simon, lyrics by Dorothy Fields, music by Cy Coleman, based on an original screenplay *Le Notte di Cabiria* by Federico Fellini, Tullio Pinelli and Ennio Flaiano, Prince of Wales Theatre, 1967. The story of a tart looking for love.
  'If my friends could see me now.'

227. *Right.* Judi Dench as Sally Bowles in *Cabaret*, a musical by Joe Masteroff, based on the play *I am a Camera* by John Van Druten and stories by Christopher Isherwood, lyrics by Fred Ebb, music by John Kander, Palace Theatre, 1968.
  'Life is a Cabaret, old chum,
  Come to the Cabaret.'

228. *Above.* John Rutland (Cook), Billy Boyle (Clerk of Oxford), Kenneth J. Warren (Miller), Daniel Thorndike (Priest), Nancy Nevinson (Nun), Pamela Charles (Prioress), Trevor Baxter (Knight), Nicky Henson (Squire), Jessie Evans (Wife of Bath), Wilfrid Brambell (Steward), Kevin Brennan (Merchant) and George Raistrick (Friar) in *Canterbury Tales*, adapted from Chaucer by Nevill Coghill and Martin Starkie, lyrics by Nevill Coghill, music by Richard Hill and John Hawkins, Phoenix Theatre, 1968.

The pilgrims dine at the Tabard Inn before setting out on their journey.

229. *Below left.* Bernard Spear as Sancho Panza and Keith Michell as Don Quixote in *Man of La Mancha*, a musical play by Dale Wasserman, lyrics by Joe Darion, music by Mitch Leigh, Piccadilly Theatre, 1968.

'I, Don Quixote . . .'

230. *Below right. Hair*, the American tribal love-rock musical by Jerome Ragni and James Rado, music by Galt MacDermot, Shaftesbury Theatre, 1968.

'OFF'

The show is over, the curtain down;
The friend is dumb or congratulates;
The tights make way for the private gown;
The cloak is on, and the carriage waits.

The carriage waits—but no longer now;
A dainty form from the door departs.
A smile perhaps, or a guarded bow,
And off she drives with a load of hearts.

1893

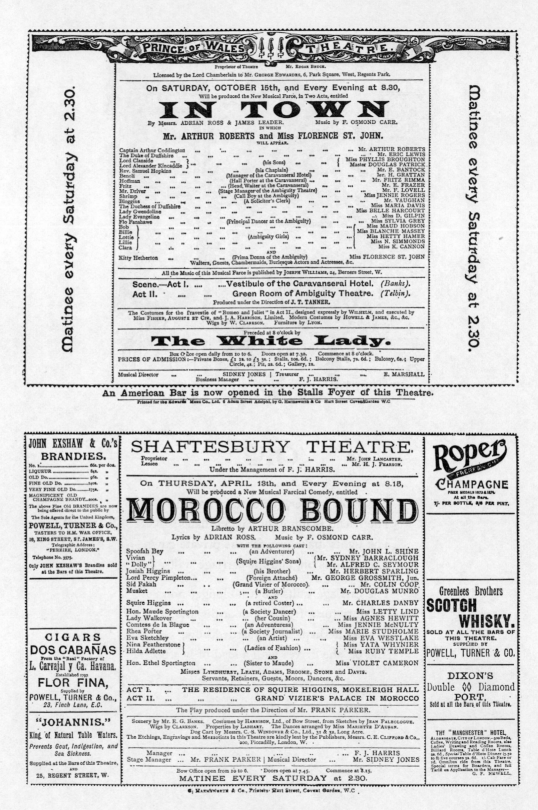

PRINCE OF WALES THEATRE.

Proprietor of Theatre   Mr. EDGAR BRUCE.

Licensed by the Lord Chamberlain to Mr. GEORGE EDWARDES, 6, Park Square, West, Regents Park.

On SATURDAY, OCTOBER 15th, and Every Evening at 8.30,
Will be produced the New Musical Farce, in Two Acts, entitled

IN TOWN

By Messrs. ADRIAN ROSS & JAMES LEADER.   Music by F. OSMOND CARR.
IN WHICH

Mr. ARTHUR ROBERTS and Miss FLORENCE ST. JOHN.
WILL APPEAR.

Captain Arthur Coddington	...	Mr. ARTHUR ROBERTS
The Duke of Duffshire	...	Mr. ERIC LEWIS
Lord Clanside	(his Sons)	Miss PHYLLIS BROUGHTON
Lord Alexander Kincaddie		Master DOUGLAS PATRICK
Rev. Samuel Hopkins	(his Chaplain)	Mr. E. BANTOCK
Benoli	(Manager of the Caravanserai Hotel)	Mr. H. GRATTAN
Hoffman	(Hall Porter at the Caravanserai)	Mr. FRITZ RIMMA
Fritz	(Head, Waiter at the Caravanserai)	Mr. E. FRAZER
Mr. Driver	(Stage Manager of the Ambiguity Theatre)	Mr. F. LOVELL
Shrimp	(Call Boy at the Ambiguity)	Miss JENNIE ROGERS
Bloggins	(A Solicitor's Clerk)	Mr. VAUGHAN
The Duchess of Duffshire	...	Miss MARIA DAVIS
Lady Gwendoline	...	Miss BELLE HARCOURT
Lady Evangeline	...	Miss D. GILPIN
Flo Fanshawe	(Principal Dancer at the Ambiguity)	Miss SYLVIA GREY
Bob	...	Miss MAUD HOBSON
Billie		Miss BLANCHE MASSEY
Lottie	(Ambiguity Girls)	Miss HETTY HAMER
Lillie		Miss N. SIMMONDS
Clara	...	Miss K. CANNON
	AND	
Kitty Hetherton	(Prima Donna of the Ambiguity)	Miss FLORENCE ST. JOHN

Waiters, Guests, Chambermaids, Burlesque Actors and Actresses, &c.

All the Music of this Musical Farce is published by JOSEPH WILLIAMS, 24, Berners Street, W.

Scene.—Act I.   ....Vestibule of the Caravanserai Hotel.   (Banks).
Act II.   Green Room of Ambiguity Theatre.   (Telbin).

Produced under the Direction of J. T. TANNER.

The Costumes for the Travestie of "Romeo and Juliet" in Act II., designed expressly by WILHELM, and executed by Miss FISHER, AUGUSTE ET CIE, and J. A. HARRISON, Limited. Modern Costumes by HOWELL & JAMES, &c., &c.
Wigs by W. CLARKSON.   Furniture by LYON.

Preceded at 8 o'clock by

The White Lady.

Box Office open daily from 10 to 6.   Doors open at 7.30.   Commence at 8 o'clock.

PRICES OF ADMISSION :—Private Boxes, £1 1s. to £3 3s. ; Stalls, 10s. 6d. ; Balcony Stalls, 7s. 6d. ; Balcony, 6s.; Upper Circle, 4s. ; Pit, 2s. 6d. ; Gallery, 1s.

Musical Director	...	SIDNEY JONES	Treasurer ... E. MARSHALL
		Business Manager ...	F. J. HARRIS.

(left margin) **Matinee every Saturday at 2.30.**

(right margin) **Matinee every Saturday at 2.30.**

SHAFTESBURY THEATRE.

Proprietor	...	Mr. JOHN LANCASTER.
Lessee	...	Mr. H. J. PEARSON.

Under the Management of F. J. HARRIS.

On THURSDAY, APRIL 13th, and Every Evening at 8.15,
Will be produced a New Musical Farcical Comedy, entitled

MOROCCO BOUND

Libretto by ARTHUR BRANSCOMBE.
Lyrics by ADRIAN ROSS.   Music by F. OSMOND CARR.

WITH THE FOLLOWING CAST :

Spoofah Bey	...	(an Adventurer)	Mr. JOHN L. SHINE
Vivian		(Squire Higgins' Sons)	Mr. SYDNEY BARRACLOUGH
"Dolly"			Mr. ALFRED C. SEYMOUR
Josiah Higgins	...	(his Brother)	Mr. HERBERT SPARLING
Lord Percy Pimpleton	...	(Foreign Attaché)	Mr. GEORGE GROSSMITH, Jun.
Sid Fakah		(Grand Vizier of Morocco).	Mr. COLIN COOP.
Musket	...	(a Butler)	Mr. DOUGLAS MUNRO
	AND		
Squire Higgins	...	(a retired Coster)	Mr. CHARLES DANBY
Hon. Maude Sportington	...	(a Society Dancer)	Miss LETTY LIND
Lady Walkover	...	(her Cousin)	Miss AGNES HEWITT
Comtess de la Blague	...	(an Adventuress)	Miss JENNIE McNULTY
Rhea Porter	...	(a Society Journalist)	Miss MARIE STUDHOLME
Eva Sketchley	...	(an Artist)	Miss EVA WESTLAKE
Nina Featherstone		(Ladies of Fashion)	Miss YATA WHYNIER
Hilda Adlette			Miss RUBY TEMPLE
	AND		
Hon. Ethel Sportington	...	(Sister to Maude)	Miss VIOLET CAMERON

Misses LYNDHURST, LEATH, ADAMS, BROOME, STONE and DAVIS.
Servants, Retainers, Guests, Moors, Dancers, &c.

ACT I.	...	THE RESIDENCE OF SQUIRE HIGGINS, MOKELEIGH HALL
ACT II.	...	GRAND VIZIER'S PALACE IN MOROCCO

The Play produced under the Direction of Mr. FRANK PARKER.

Scenery by Mr. E. G. BANKS.   Costumes by HARRISON, Ltd., of Bow Street, from Sketches by JEAN PALEOLOGUE.
Wigs by CLARKSON.   Properties by LABHART.   The Dances arranged by Miss MARIETTE D'AUBAN.
Dog Cart by Messrs. C. S. WINDOVER & Co., Ltd., 31 & 32, Long Acre.
The Etchings, Engravings and Mezzotints in this Theatre are kindly lent by the Publishers, Messrs. C. E. CLIFFORD & Co., 200, Piccadilly, London, W.

Manager	...		... F. J. HARRIS
Stage Manager	...	Mr. FRANK PARKER	Musical Director ... Mr. SIDNEY JONES

Bow Office open from 10 to 6.   Doors open at 7.45.   Commence at 8.15.

MATINEE EVERY SATURDAY at 2.30.

G. HARMSWORTH & Co., Printers, Hart Street, Covent Garden, W.C.

PRINCE OF WALES THEATRE.

Mr. GEORGE EDWARDES

WILL PRODUCE

On SATURDAY, OCTOBER 14th, at 8.20, a New Musical Comedy, entitled

A GAIETY GIRL.

Words by OWEN HALL.   Lyrics by HARRY GREENBANK.   Music by SIDNEY JONES.

Charles Goldfield	(Captain in the IX. Life Guards)	Mr. C. HAYDEN COFFIN
		(His First Appearance since his return from America.)
Major Barclay		Mr. FRED KAYE
Bobbie Rivers		Mr. W. LOUIS BRADFIELD
Harry Fitzwarren	(Officers of the IX. Life Guards)	Mr. LEEDHAM BANTOCK
Romney Farquhar		Mr. LAWRANCE D'ORSAY
Sir Alfred Grey	(a Judge of the Divorce Court)	Mr. ERIC LEWIS
Lance		Mr. GILBERT PORTEOUS
Auguste	(a Bathing Attendant)	Mr. FRITZ RIMMA
	AND	
Rev. Montague Brierly	(Hon. Chaplain to the IX. Life Guards)	Mr. HARRY MONKHOUSE
Rose Brierly	(his Daughter)	Miss DECIMA MOORE
Lady Edytha Aldwyn		Miss KATE CUTLER
Miss Gladys Stourton	(Society Ladies)	Miss MARIE STUDHOLME
Hon. Daisy Ormsbury		Miss LOUIE POUNDS
Lady Grey		Mrs. E. PHELPS
Alma Somerset		Miss MAUD HOBSON
Cissy Verner		Miss BLANCHE MASSEY
Haidee Walton	(Gaiety Girls)	Miss ROSS SELWICK
Ethel Hawthorne		Miss VIOLET ROBINSON
Mina	(a French Maid)	Miss JULIETTE NESVILLE
	AND	
Lady Virginia Forest		Miss LOTTIE VENNE

ACT I. ... ... THE CAVALRY BARRACKS AT WINBRIDGE (*W. Hann*)
ACT II. ... ... ON THE RIVIERA (*W. Telbin*)

MATINEE EVERY SATURDAY at 2.30

PRICES.—Boxes, £1 1s to £4 4s. Orchestra Stalls, 10s. 6d.; Balcony Stalls (First Two Rows), 7s. 6d.; Other Rows, 6s.; Upper Circle, 4s.; (Numbered and Reserved); Pit, 2s. 6d.; Gallery, 1s.   Doors open at 8.   Box Office open daily from 10 till 5.

The Dresses by Miss FISHER, AUGUSTE, HARRISONS, Ltd., and ALIAS, from Designs by EDEL.   The Modern Costumes by DEBENHAM, FREEBODY, MOUKOPF, &c.   Uniforms by MORRIS ANGEL, &c.

PIANOS KINDLY LENT BY MESSRS. ERARD, GREAT MARLBOROUGH STREET.

Musical Director, Mr. SIDNEY JONES.   Stage Manager, Mr. J. A. E. MALONE.   Acting Manager, Mr. C. P. LEVILLY

PROPRIETOR, MR. EDGAR BRUCE.

GAIETY THEATRE.

LESSEE AND MANAGER ---- GEORGE EDWARDES.

To-night, and Every Evening at 8,
DOORS OPEN AT 7.40,
MR. GEORGE EDWARDES will produce

THE SHOP GIRL,

A MUSICAL FARCE,

By H. J. W. DAM.   Music by IVAN CARYLL.
Additional Numbers by ADRIAN ROSS & LIONEL MONCKTON.

Mr. Hooley	(Proprietor of the Royal Stores)	Mr. ARTHUR WILLIAMS
Charles Appleby	(A Medical Student)	Mr. SEYMOUR HICKS
Bertie Boyd	(One of the Boys)	Mr. GEORGE GROSSMITH, Junr.
John Brown	(A Millionaire)	Mr. COLIN COOP
Sir George Appleby	(A Solicitor)	Mr. CAIRNS JAMES
Col. Singleton	(Retired)	Mr. FRANK WHEELER
Count St. Vaurien	(Secretary to Mr. Brown)	Mr. ROBERT ROBINSON
Mr. Tweets	(Financial Secretary to Lady Appleby)	Mr. WILLIE WARDE
	AND	
Mr. Miggles	(Shopwalker at the Royal Stores)	Mr. EDMUND PAYNE
Lady Dodo Singleton	(Charlie's Cousin)	Miss MAUD SHERMAN
Miss Robinson	(Fitter at the Royal Stores)	Miss KATIE SEYMOUR
Lady Appleby	(Charlie's Mother, Wife of Sir George)	Miss MARIA DAVIS
Ada Smith	(An Apprentice at the Royal Stores)	Miss LILLIE BELMORE
Faith		Miss LILLIE DICKINSON
Hope	Lady Appleby's Daughters	Miss AGATHA ROZE
Charity		Miss LILY JOHNSON
Maud Plantagenet		Miss MAUD HILL
Eva Tudor		Miss FANNIE WARDE
Lillie Stuart		Miss MAUD SUTHERLAND
Ada Wandesforde		Miss HELEN LEE
Mabel Beresford	of the Syndicate Theatre	Miss VIOLET MONCKTON
Agnes Howard		Miss LOUIE COOTE
Maggie Jocelyn		Miss MAGGIE RIPLEY
Violet Tierney		Miss TOPSY SINDEN
	AND	
Bessie Brent	("The Shop Girl")	Miss ADA REEVE

Act I.—The Royal Stores (*W. Johnstone*).   Act II.—Fancy Bazaar at Kensington (*W. Hann*).
PAS SEUL, in the Second Act, by Miss TOPSY SINDEN.

Dances arranged by WILLIE WARDE.   Costumes designed by WILHELM, and executed by Miss FISHER, Madame AUGUSTE, HARRISONS, Limited, and MORRIS ANGEL.   Wigs by C. H. FOX.   Furniture, &c., by OETZMANN & Co., Hampstead Road, N.W.

Stage Director ... ... J. T. TANNER
Acting Manager ... ... E. MARSHALL

PRICES OF ADMISSION.—Private Boxes, 1 to 4 Guineas; Orchestra Stalls, 10s. 6d.; Balcony Stalls, 1st and 2nd Rows, 7s.; 3rd and 4th Rows, 6s.; Upper Boxes (Numbered and Reserved) 4s.; Pit, 2s. 6d.; Gallery, 1s.

Doors open at 7.40.   Box Office open daily from 10 to 6. under the direction of A. P. OXLEY.

G. HARMSWORTH & Co., GENERAL PRINTERS, ETC., 42, HART STREET, COVENT GARDEN.   24-11-94

Musicals which have run 500 performances and over in London 1894-1968

The New York run (if any), before or after London, is also given

Name	LONDON Theatre and date	Perfs	NEW YORK New York theatre and date	Perfs
OLIVER	New Theatre 30 June 1960	2,618	Imperial Theatre 6 January 1963	774
THE SOUND OF MUSIC	Palace Theatre 18 May 1961	2,386	Lunt-Fontanne Theatre 16 November 1959	1,443
SALAD DAYS	Vaudeville Theatre 5 August 1954	2,283	Barbizon Plaza Theatre 10 November 1958	80
MY FAIR LADY	Theatre Royal, Drury Lane 30 April 1958	2,281	Mark Hellinger Theatre 15 March 1956	2,717
CHU CHIN CHOW	His Majesty's Theatre 31 August 1916	2,238	Manhattan Opera House 22 October 1917	208
THE BOY FRIEND	Wyndham's Theatre 14 January 1954	2,084	Royale Theatre 30 September 1954	485
ME AND MY GIRL	Victoria Palace 16 December 1937	1,646		
OKLAHOMA!	Theatre Royal, Drury Lane 30 April 1947	1,543	St James Theatre 31 March 1943	2,248
IRMA LA DOUCE	Lyric Theatre 17 July 1958	1,512	Plymouth Theatre 29 September 1960	524
THE MAID OF THE MOUNTAINS	Daly's Theatre 10 February 1917	1,352	Casino Theatre 11 September 1918	37
ANNIE GET YOUR GUN	Coliseum 7 June 1947	1,304	Imperial Theatre 16 May 1946	1,147
A CHINESE HONEYMOON	Royal Strand Theatre 5 October 1901	1,075	Casino Theatre 2 June 1902	376
WEST SIDE STORY	Her Majesty's Theatre 12 December 1958	1,040	Winter Garden Theatre 26 September 1957	732
PERCHANCE TO DREAM	London Hippodrome 21 April 1945	1,022		
THE DANCING YEARS (Revival)	Adelphi Theatre 19 March 1942 Originally produced at Drury Lane, 23 March 1939, withdrawn at outbreak of war—187 performances	969		

	LONDON			NEW YORK	
Name	*Theatre and date*	*Perfs*	*New York theatre and date*		*Perfs*
ROBERT AND ELIZABETH	Lyric Theatre 20 October 1964	948			
THE KING AND I	Theatre Royal, Drury Lane 8 October 1953	946	St James Theatre 29 March 1951		1,246
FINGS AIN'T WOT THEY USED T' BE	Garrick Theatre, 11 February 1960 First produced at the Theatre Royal, Stratford 22 December 1959	886			
BLESS THE BRIDE	Adelphi Theatre 26 April 1947	886			
ROSE MARIE	Theatre Royal, Drury Lane 20 March 1926	851	Imperial Theatre 2 September 1924		581
KING'S RHAPSODY	Palace Theatre 15 September 1949	841			
THE ARCADIANS	Shaftesbury Theatre 28 April 1909	809	Liberty Theatre 17 January 1910		136
THE BOY	Adelphi Theatre 14 September 1917	801			
HELLO, DOLLY!	Theatre Royal, Drury Lane 2 December 1965	794	St James Theatre 16 January 1964		Still running
SOUTH PACIFIC	Theatre Royal, Drury Lane 1 November 1951	792	Majestic Theatre 7 April 1949		1,830
THE MERRY WIDOW	Daly's Theatre 8 June 1907	778	New Amsterdam Theatre 21 October 1907		416
SAN TOY	Daly's Theatre 21 October 1899	768	Daly's Theatre 1 October 1900		65
A FUNNY THING HAPPENED ON THE WAY TO THE FORUM	Strand Theatre 3 October 1963	762	Alvin Theatre 8 May 1962		966
THE GEISHA	Daly's Theatre 25 April 1896	760	Daly's Theatre 9 September 1896		161
A COUNTRY GIRL	Daly's Theatre 18 January 1902	729	Daly's Theatre 22 September 1902		112
THE BELLE OF NEW YORK	Shaftesbury Theatre 12 April 1898	697	Casino Theatre 28 September 1897		56
BITTER-SWEET	His Majesty's Theatre 18 July 1929	697	Ziegfeld Theatre 5 November 1929		159

	LONDON		NEW YORK	
Name	*Theatre and date*	*Perfs*	*New York theatre and date*	*Perfs*
PICKWICK	Saville Theatre *4 July 1963*	694	46th Street Theatre *4 October 1965*	56
BRIGADOON	His Majesty's Theatre *14 April 1949*	685	Ziegfeld Theatre *13 March 1947*	581
HALF A SIXPENCE	Cambridge Theatre *21 March 1963*	678	Broadhurst Theatre *25 April 1965*	512
THE TOREADOR	Gaiety Theatre *17 June 1901*	675	Knickerbocker Theatre *6 January 1902*	146
GRAB ME A GONDOLA	Lyric Theatre *26 December 1956* First produced at the Lyric, Hammersmith *27 November 1956*	673		
NO, NO, NANETTE	Palace Theatre *11 March 1925*	665	Globe Theatre *16 September 1925*	329
UNDER THE COUNTER	Phoenix Theatre *22 November 1945*	665	Shubert Theatre *3 October 1947*	27
BLUE FOR A BOY	His Majesty's Theatre *30 November 1950*	664		
LOCK UP YOUR DAUGHTERS (Revival and transfer)	Mermaid Theatre *17 May 1962*, transferred to Her Majesty's Theatre *16 August 1962* Originally produced at the Mermaid Theatre *28 May 1959* 328 performances	664	Pre Broadway tour opened Shubert Theatre, New Haven, Conn. *27 April 1960* —Closed 7 May. Shubert Theatre, Boston	
WHITE HORSE INN	Coliseum *8 April 1931*	651	Center Theatre *1 October 1936*	211
KISMET	Stoll Theatre *20 April 1955*	648	Ziegfeld Theatre *3 December 1953*	583
OUR MISS GIBBS	Gaiety Theatre *23 January 1909*	636	Knickerbocker Theatre *29 August 1910*	64
YES, UNCLE!	Prince of Wales Theatre *29 December 1917*	626		
LILAC TIME	Lyric Theatre *22 December 1922*	626	American version *Blossom Time* (from same original) 1921	
THE CATCH OF THE SEASON	Vaudeville Theatre *9 September 1904*	621	Daly's Theatre *28 August 1905*	104
WALTZES FROM VIENNA	Alhambra Theatre *17 August 1931*	607	American version *The Great Waltz* (from the same original) 1934	

[42]

	LONDON			NEW YORK	
Name	Theatre and date	Perfs		New York theatre and date	Perfs
LOVE FROM JUDY	Saville Theatre 25 September 1952	594			
A RUNAWAY GIRL	Gaiety Theatre 21 May 1898	593		Daly's Theatre 25 August 1898	212
THE PAJAMA GAME	Coliseum 13 October 1955	578		St James Theatre 13 May 1954	1,061
FOLLOW THE GIRLS	His Majesty's Theatre 25 October 1945	572		Century Theatre 8 April 1944	882
BALALAIKA	Adelphi Theatre 22 December 1936	570			
BLITZ!	Adelphi Theatre 8 May 1962	567			
CAROUSEL	Theatre Royal, Drury Lane 7 June 1950	566		Majestic Theatre 19 April 1945	890
THE BING BOYS ON BROADWAY	Alhambra Theatre 16 February 1918	562			
THE ORCHID	Gaiety Theatre 26 October 1903	559		Herald Square Theatre 8 April 1907	178
GUYS AND DOLLS	Coliseum 28 May 1953	555		46th Street Theatre 24 November 1950	1,194
THE SHOP GIRL	Gaiety Theatre 24 November 1894	546		Palmer's Theatre 28 October 1895	72
ZIP GOES A MILLION	Palace Theatre 20 October 1951	544			
THE QUAKER GIRL	Adelphi Theatre 5 November 1910	536		Park Theatre 23 October 1911	240
MR. CINDERS	Adelphi Theatre 11 February 1929	528			
HOW TO SUCCEED IN IN BUSINESS WITHOUT REALLY TRYING	Shaftesbury Theatre (late Princes) 28 March 1963	520		46th Street Theatre 14 October 1961	1,417
CAMELOT	Theatre Royal, Drury Lane 19 August 1964	518		Majestic Theatre 3 December 1960	873
UNDER YOUR HAT	Palace Theatre 24 November 1938	512			

	LONDON			NEW YORK	
Name	*Theatre and date*	*Perfs*		*New York theatre and date*	*Perfs*
KATJA, THE DANCER	Gaiety Theatre *21 February 1925*	505		44th Street Theatre *18 October 1926*	112
THEODORE AND CO	Gaiety Theatre *19 September 1916*	503			
GAY'S THE WORD	Saville Theatre *16 February 1951*	502			
MAGGIE MAY	Adelphi Theatre *22 September 1964*	501			

STILL RUNNING, 31 DECEMBER 1968

CHARLIE GIRL	Adelphi Theatre *15 December 1965*				
FIDDLER ON THE ROOF	Her Majesty's Theatre *16 February 1967*			Imperial Theatre *22 September 1964* (still running)	
THE FOUR MUSKETEERS	Theatre Royal, Drury Lane *5 December 1967* (run ended 18 January 1969)				
CANTERBURY TALES	Phoenix Theatre *21 March 1968*			Eugene O'Neill Theatre *3 February 1969*	
HAIR	Shaftesbury Theatre *27 September 1968*			New York Shakespeare Festival Public Theatre *17 October 1967* Transferred to The Cheetah, *22 December 1967* Broadway production Biltmore Theatre, *29 April 1968* (still running)	
MR. AND MRS.	Palace Theatre *11 December 1968* (run ended 18 January 1969)				
THE YOUNG VISITERS	Piccadilly Theatre *23 December 1968* (run ended 15 February 1969)				

Indexes

(The numbers refer throughout to picture captions only)

MUSICALS Illustrated

The names of the authors, lyricists and composers are included in the captions, and indexed in the following pages. The names in this list are of (I) Director, (II) Designer of sets and costume, (III) Choreographer—when credited on the original programme.

[45]

	(I)	(II)	(III)
CHU CHIN CHOW 108, 109, 110	Oscar Asche	(S) *Joseph and Phil Harker* (C) *Percy Anderson*	*Espinosa*
CINEMA STAR, THE 102, 103	Robert Courtneidge	(S) *R. C. McCleery and Conrad Tritschler* (C) *Reville, Herbert Norris and Lucile*	*Espinosa*
CINGALEE, THE 51		(S) *Hawes Craven* (C) *Percy Anderson*	*Willie Warde*
CIRCUS GIRL, THE 10, 11		(S) *T. E. Ryan and William Telbin* (C) *Comelli*	*Willie Warde*
CLO-CLO 133	Dion Titheradge	(S) *Marc Henri and Laverdet* (C) *Idare, Lichtowier and Marc Henri*	*Max Rivers*
COME SPY WITH ME 223	Ned Sherrin	(S) *Disley Jones* (C) *Mark Canter*	*Irving Davis*
CONVERSATION PIECE 176	Noël Coward	(S) & (C) *G. E. Calthrop*	
COUNT OF LUX- EMBOURG, THE 89, 90	Edward Royce	(S) *Alfred Terraine* (C) *Comelli*	*Edward Royce*
COUNTRY GIRL, A 38, 39		(S) *Hawes Craven and Joseph Harker* (C) *Percy Anderson*	*Willie Warde*
DAIRYMAIDS, THE 57, 58	Robert Courtneidge	(S) *Conrad Tritschler and R. C. McCleery* (C) *Wilhelm*	*Harry Grattan*
DANCING YEARS, THE 188	Leontine Sagan	(S) *Joseph Carl, Edward Delany and Alick Johnstone* (C) *Frederick Denison and Louis Brooks*	*Freddie Carpenter and Suria Magito*
DESERT SONG, THE 145	Laurence Schwab	(S) *Joseph and Phil Harker* (C) *Robert E. Groves*	*Robert Connolly*
DOLLAR PRIN- CESS, THE 82, 83	Edward Royce	(S) *Alfred Terraine and Joseph Harker* (C) *Lucile and Comelli*	
EARL AND THE GIRL, THE 46	Seymour Hicks	(S) *W. Harford* (C) *Comelli, Mayhum and Courtnay*	*Edward Royce, Jr*

	(I)	(II)	(III)
EVER GREEN 164	Frank Collins	(S) *G. E. Calthrop, Rex Whistler, Marc Henri and Laverdet, Ernst Stern and Gustavo Bacarisis* (C) *Reville, Ernst Stern, Ada Peacock and Doris Zinkeisen*	*Buddy Bradley and Billy Pierce*
FIDDLER ON THE ROOF 225	Jerome Robbins	(S) *Boris Aronson* (C) *Patricia Zipprodt*	*Jerome Robbins*
FINGS AIN'T WOT THEY USED T' BE 216	Joan Littlewood	(S) & (C) *John Bury*	
FLORODORA 28, 29	Sydney Ellison	(S) *Julian Hicks* (C) *Comelli*	
FOLLOW A STAR 160	Jack Hulbert	(S) *Lyndhurst* (C) *Busvines*	*Guy de Gerald*
FUNNY FACE 157, 158	Felix Edwardes	(S) *Joseph and Phil Harker and Prince Galitzine* (C) *Jenny and Reville*	*Robert Connolly*
GAIETY GIRL, A 5, 6		(S) *Walter Hann and William Telbin* (C) *Edel and Redfern*	
GAY DIVORCE 175	Felix Edwardes	(S) *Joseph and Phil Harker* (C) *Betty Boor*	*Carl Randall and Barbara Newberry*
GAY PARISIENNE, THE 16, 17	Horace Sedger	(S) *E. G. Banks and William Telbin* (C) *Comelli*	*Will Bishop*
GAY GORDONS, THE 63	Seymour Hicks	(S) *R. C. McCleery* (C) *Wilhelm*	*Edward Royce*
GEISHA, THE 14		(S) *William Telbin* (C) *Percy Anderson*	*Willie Warde*
GENTLEMAN JOE (THE HANSOM CABBY) 20	Hugh Moss	(S) *Joseph Harker and T. E .Ryan* (C) —	*Willie Warde*
GENTLEMEN PREFER BLONDES 217	Henry Kaplan	(S) *Hutchinson Scott* (C) *Hilary Virgo and Rosemary Carvill*	*Ralph Beaumont*
GIRL BEHIND THE COUNTER, THE 59	Frank Curzon and Austen Hurgon	(S) *Julian Hicks* (C) *Karl, etc.*	
GIRL BEHIND THE GUN, THE see KISSING TIME			
GIRL FRIEND, THE (KITTY'S KISSES) 148	William Mollison	(S) *F. L. Lyndhurst and Phil Harker* (C) *Reville*	*Max Scheck*

	(I)	(II)	(III)
GIRL FROM KAY'S, THE 42		(S) *Joseph Harker and W. B. Spong* (C) *Wilhelm*	*Willie Warde*
GIRL FROM UTAH, THE 96	J. A. E. Malone	(S) *T. E. Ryan, Alfred Terraine, Hawes Craven and Joseph Hunter* (C) *Comelli*	*Willie Warde and Will Bishop*
GIRL IN THE TAXI, THE 94	Michael Faraday	(S) & (C) *Baruch & Co.*	
GIRL ON THE FILM, THE 98, 99	George Edwardes	(S) *Alfred Terraine and J. E. Ryan* (C) *Comelli*	
GIRLS OF GOTTENBERG, THE 64	J. A. E. Malone	(S) *Alfred Terraine and Joseph and Phil Harker* (C) *Percy Anderson*	*Fred Farren*
GLAMOROUS NIGHT 177, 178	Leontine Sagan	(S) & (C) *Oliver Messel*	*Ralph Reader*
GOING GREEK 182	Leslie Henson and Herbert Bryan	(S) & (C) *René Hubert*	*Jack Donohue*
GOING UP 115	William J. Wilson	(S) *T. E. Ryan and Owen* (C) *Idare, Lichtowier and Marc Henri*	*James L. Lester*
GREEK SLAVE, A 21, 22, 23		(S) *Joseph Harker and T. E. Ryan* (C) *Percy Anderson*	*Willie Warde*
HAIR 230	Tom O'Horgan	(S) *Robin Wagner* (C) *Nancy Potts*	*Julie Arenal*
HALF A SIXPENCE 218	John Dexter	(S) & (C) *Loudon Sainthill*	*Edmund Balin*
HAPPY DAY, THE 112	Edward Royce	(S) *E. H. Ryan, Alfred Terraine and Joseph Harker* (C) *Comelli and Esther*	
HAVANA 69, 70	George Edwardes	(S) *Joseph Harker and Alfred Terraine* (C) *Percy Anderson*	*Edward Royce*
HEADS UP! 162	Harry Howell	(S) *Joseph and Phil Harker* (C) *Idare*	*Elsie Neal*
HELLO, DOLLY! 222	Gower Champion	(S) *Oliver Smith* (C) *Freddy Wittop*	*Gower Champion*
HIDE AND SEEK 184	Jack Hulbert	(S) *David Holman* (C) *Alec Shanks, etc.*	*Jack Hulbert*
HIT THE DECK 149	William Mollison	(S) *F. L. Lyndhurst* (C) *Reville, etc.*	*Max Scheck*

	(I)	(II)	(III)
HOLD MY HAND 167	Stanley Lupino	(S) *F. L. Lyndhurst* (C) *Idare*	*Buddy Bradley*
IN DAHOMEY 43, 44	Jesse A. Shipp		
IN TOWN 2, 3	James T. Tanner	(S) *William Telbin and Banks* (C) —	*Mariette D'Auban*
IRENE 119	Tom Reynolds	(S) *Alfred Terraine, E. H. Ryan and Raphael* (C) *Stein and Blaine, Reneaux, etc.*	
JILL, DARLING! 174	William Mollison	(S) *Leon Davey* (C) *Norman Hartnell, Rubens, etc.*	*Fred Lord*
KATJA, THE DANCER 131, 132	Fred J. Blackman	(S) *Alfred Terraine and Joseph and Phil Harker* (C) *Comelli*	
KING AND I 203	John van Druten	(S) *Jo Mielziner* (C) *Irene Sharaff*	*Jerome Robbins*
KING OF CADONIA 75, 76	Frank Curzon	(S) *Hawes Craven* (C) *Karl*	
KING'S RHAPSODY 197	Murray Macdonald	(S) *Edward Delany* (C) *Frederick Dawson*	*Pauline Grant*
KISMET 208	Albert Marre	(S) *Lemuel Ayers* (C) —	*Jack Cole*
KISS ME, KATE 201	Sam Spewack	(S) *Lemuel Ayers* (C) —	*Hanya Holm*
KISSING TIME (GIRL BEHIND THE GUN, THE) 117	Felix Edwardes	(S) *Rousin, Marc Henri and Laverdet* (C) *Comelli, St Martin and Idare*	*Cissie Sewell*
KITTY GREY 34		(S) *W. B. Spong* (C) —	
KITTY'S KISSES (see GIRL FRIEND, THE) 148			
LADY, BE GOOD! 142	Felix Edwardes	(S) *Joseph and Phil Harker* (C) *Idare*	*Max Scheck*
LADY MADCAP 56	J. A. E. Malone	(S) *Hawes Craven and Joseph Harker* (C) *Percy Anderson*	*Willie Warde*
LADY OF THE ROSE, THE 126	Fred J. Blackman	(S) *Joseph Harker and Alfred Terraine* (C) *Comelli and Esther*	*A. H. Majilton*
LADY SLAVEY, THE 12	George Dance	(S) *E. G. Banks* (C) —	*Mariette D'Auban*

[50]

	(I)	(II)	(III)
LAND OF SMILES, THE 169	Felix Edwardes	(S) *Alick Johnstone* (C) *Therese and Kaufmann*	
LILAC TIME 122	Dion Boucicault	(S) *E. H. Ryan* (C) *Comelli*	*Carlotta Mossetti*
LISBON STORY, THE 189	George Black and Alexander Marsh	(S) & (C) *George Ramon*	*Wendy Toye*
LOCK UP YOUR DAUGHTERS 212	Peter Coe	(S) & (C) *Sean Kenny*	*Gilbert Vernon*
LORD TOM NODDY 15	George Dance	(S) *Henry Enden and W. Harford* (C) *Comelli*	*Will Bishop*
LOVE FROM JUDY 202	Charles Hickman	(S) & (C) *Berkeley Sutcliffe*	*Pauline Grant*
LOVE LIES 159	Stanley Lupino and Arthur Rigby	(S) *Rudolf Haybrook* (C) *Irene Segalla*	*Fred Lord*
MADAME POMPADOUR 125	Fred J. Blackman	(S) *Alfred Terraine, Joseph and Phil Harker* (C) *Comelli*	*A. H. Majilton*
MAID OF THE MOUNTAINS, THE 114	Oscar Asche	(S) *Joseph Harker* (C) *Comelli*	
MAN OF LA MANCHA 229	Albert Marre	(S) *Howard Bay* (C) *Howard Bay and Patton Campbell*	*Jack Cole*
MARRIAGE MARKET, THE 100, 101	Edward Royce	(S) *E. H. Ryan and Alfred Terraine* (C) *Comelli*	*Espinosa*
ME AND MY GIRL 183	Lupino Lane	(S) *Edward Delaney* (C) *Louis Brooks, etc.*	*Fred Leslie*
MEDAL AND THE MAID, THE 36	Sydney Ellison	(S) *Walter Hann and T. E. Ryan* (C) *Comelli*	*Larry Ceballos*
MERCENARY MARY 141	William Mollison	(S) *F. L. Lyndhurst* (C) *Idare, etc.*	*Fred Farren*
MERRY WIDOW, THE 66, 67, 68	J. E. A. Malone	(S) *Alfred Terraine and Joseph Harker* (C) *Lucile Pascaud and Percy Anderson*	
MESSENGER BOY, THE 30		(S) *Joseph Harker and T. E. Ryan* (C) *Wilhelm*	*Willie Warde*
MISS HOOK OF HOLLAND 60	Austen Hurgon	(S) *Joseph Harker and Walter Hann* (C) *Karl*	
MOROCCO BOUND 4	Frank Parker	(S) *E. G. Banks* (C) *Jean Paleoloque*	*Mariette D'Auban*

	(I)	(II)	(III)
MOUSMÉ, THE 91	Robert Courtneidge	(S) *Conrad Tritschler* (C) *Wilhelm*	*Roy Mack, Fred A. Leslie and Charles Brooks*
MR. CINDERS 161	George G. Parker	(S) *Joseph and Phil Harker* (C) —	
MR. WHITTINGTON 175	Jack Buchanan	(S) *Aubrey Hammond* (C) *Idare*	*Jack Donohue and Jack Buchanan*
MY DARLING 65	Seymour Hicks	(S) *R. C. McCleery and Walter Hann* (C) *Comelli, Lucile, etc.*	*Edward Royce*
MY FAIR LADY 209	Moss Hart	(S) *Oliver Smith* (C) *Cecil Beaton*	*Hanya Holm*
MY MIMOSA MAID 71	Austen Hurgon	(S) *Hawes Craven and Walter Hann* (C) *Karl*	
NEW MOON, THE 154	Felix Edwardes	(S) *Joseph and Phil Harker and Prince Galitzine* (C) *Irene Segalla*	*Robert Connolly*
NO, NO, NANETTE 138, 139, 140	William Mollison	(S) *F. H. Lyndhurst* (C) *Peron and Idare*	*C. A. Leonard*
NYMPH ERRANT 172	Romney Brent	(S) & (C) *Doris Zinkeisen*	*Agnes de Mille, Carl Randall and Barbara Newberry*
OH, JOY! (OH, BOY!) 116	Austen Hurgon	(S) *J. A. Fraser* (C) *St Martin and Hockley*	*Harry French and Hylda Lewis*
OH, KAY! 144	William Potter	(S) *Phil Harker* (C) *Idare and Guy de Gerald*	*Sammy Lee*
OH! OH!! DELPHINE!!! 95	George A. Highland	(S) *R. C. McCleery, Walter Hann and Conrad Tritschler* (C) *Martial, Armand et Cie, Herbert Norris, Redfern and Reville*	
OH! YOU LETTY 185	Campbell Gullan	(S) *Clifford Pember* (C) —	*Philip Buchel and Dimitri Vladmiroff*
OKLAHOMA! 194	Rouben Mamoulian	(S) *Lemuel Ayres* (C) *Miles White*	*Agnes de Mille*
OLIVER 213	Peter Coe	(S) *Sean Kenny* (C) —	

	(I)	(II)	(III)
ON YOUR TOES 180	Leslie Henson	(S) *The Harkers* (C) *Betty Boor*	*Andy Anderson and George Balanchine*
OPERETTE 186	Noël Coward	(S) & (C) *G. E. Calthrop*	*Cissie Sewell*
ORCHID, THE 47, 48, 49	Sydney Ellison	(S) *Hawes Craven* (C) *Wilhelm*	
OUR MISS GIBBS 77, 78	George Edwardes and Edward Royce	(S) *Joseph Harker* (C) *Comelli*	*Edward Royce*
PAL JOEY 207	Neil Hartley	(S) *Oliver Smith* (C) *Miles White*	*Robert Alton*
PANAMA HATTIE 190	William Mollison	(S) *Clifford Pember* (C) *Norman Hartnell, etc.*	*Wendy Toye*
PEARL GIRL, THE 97	Robert Courtneidge	(S) *Conrad Tritschler and R. C. McCleery* (C) *Herbert Norris, Reville, Martial, Armand et Cie*	*Willie Warde and Espinosa*
PEGGY 87, 88	George Edwardes	(S) *Joseph Harker* (C) *Comelli*	*Edward Royce*
PERCHANCE TO DREAM 192	Jack Minster	(S) *Joseph Carl* (C) *F. Dawson*	*Frank Staff*
PICKWICK 219	Peter Coe	(S) *Sean Kenny* (C) *Roger Furse*	*Leo Kharibian*
PLEASE, TEACHER! 179	Ralph Reader	(S) *Clifford Pember* (C) *Claire Avis Taishoffer*	*Ralph Reader*
PRINCE OF PILSEN, THE 50	George Marion	(S) *Walter Burridge* (C) *Will R. Barnes and Archie Gunn*	
PRINCESS CAPRICE 93	William Mollison	(S) *F. L. Lyndhurst and Gordon Conway* (C) *Elspeth Fox-Pitt, Percy Anderson, etc.*	*Espinosa and Kelland Espinosa*
PRINCESS CHARMING 143	Robert Courtneidge	(S) *Conrad Tritschler* (C) *Martial, Armand et Cie and Herbert Norris*	*Espinosa*
QUAKER GIRL, THE 86	J. A. E. Malone	(S) *Joseph Harker, A. Terraine and Paquereau* (C) *Percy Anderson and Alexandra*	*Willie Warde*
RIO RITA 163	John Harwood	(S) — (C) *Idare, etc.*	*Edward Royce, Jr., and Alexander Oumansky*
ROBERT AND ELIZABETH 221	Wendy Toye	(S) & (C) *Malcolm Pride*	*Wendy Toye*

	(I)	(II)	(III)
ROSE MARIE 136, 137	Felix Edwardes	(S) *Joseph and Phil Harker* (C) *Comelli*	*J. Kathryn Scott*
RUNAWAY GIRL, A 18, 19		(S) *Joseph Harker and T. E. Ryan* (C) *Wilhelm*	*Willie Warde*
SAIL AWAY 215	Noël Coward	(S) & (C) *Loudon Sainthill*	*Joe Layton*
SALAD DAYS 206	Denis Carey	(S) *Patrick Robertson* (C) *Alvary Williams*	*Elizabeth West*
SALLY 121	George Grossmith	(S) *Joseph and Phil Harker* (C) *Idare, Lucile and Alias*	*Jack Haskell*
SAN TOY 27	Richard Barker	(S) *Hawes Craven and Joseph Harker* (C) *Percy Anderson*	*Willie Warde*
SCHOOL GIRL, THE 40, 41		(S) *Hawes Craven and Joseph Harker* (C) *Percy Anderson*	*Willie Warde*
SHOP GIRL, THE 7, 8, 9	James T. Tanner	(S) *W. Johnstone and Walter Hann* (C) *Wilhelm*	*Willie Warde*
SHOW BOAT 153	Felix Edwardes	(S) *Joseph and Phil Harker* (C) *Irene Segalla*	*Max Scheck*
SO THIS IS LOVE 151, 152	Leslie Henson	(S) *Joseph and Phil Harker* (C) *Idare*	*Max Rivers*
SOUND OF MUSIC, THE 214	Jerome Whyte	(S) *Oliver Smith* (C) *Lucinda Ballard*	*Joe Layton*
SOUTH PACIFIC 200	Joshua Logan	(S) *Jo Mielziner* (C) *Motley*	
STOP FLIRTING! 134	Felix Edwardes	(S) *Phil Harker* (C) *Idare, etc.*	*Gus Sohlke*
STREET SINGER, THE 129	E. Lyall Swete	(S) *Joseph and Phil Harker* (C) *Idare and Dolly Tree*	*Fred A. Leslie*
SUNNY 146	Charles Mast	(S) *Joseph and Phil Harker* (C) *Idare, etc.*	
SUNSHINE GIRL, THE 92	George Edwardes and J. A. E. Malone	(S) *Alfred Terraine and Joseph Harker* (C) *Comelli*	*Willie Warde*
SWEET CHARITY 226	Bob Fosse	(S) *Robert Randolph* (C) *Irene Sharaff*	*Bob Fosse*

		(I)	(II)	(III)
SYBIL	120	Seymour Hicks	(S) *E. H. Ryan, Joseph and Phil Harker and Alfred Terraine* (C) *Comelli, Reville and Esther*	*Fred Farren*
TELL HER THE TRUTH	171	William Mollison	(S) *F. H. Lyndhurst* (C) *Reville*	*Fred Leslie*
TELL ME MORE	135	Felix Edwardes	(S) *Joseph and Phil Harker* (C) *Comelli, Christabel Russell and Idare*	*Sammy Lee*
THAT'S A GOOD GIRL	150	Jack Buchanan	(S) *F. H. Lyndhurst and Marc-Henri* (C) *Idare*	*Jack Buchanan, Anton Dolin and Dave Fitzgibbon*
THEODORE & CO.	107	Austen Hurgon	(S) *Joseph and Phil Harker and Alfred Craven* (C) *Poiret, Phelps and Lucile*	*Gwladys Dillon*
THREE GRACES, THE	128	Tom Reynolds	(S) *Joseph and Phil Harker and H. Humphries* (C) *Comelli and Idare*	*J. W. Jackson*
TINA	104	Edward Royce	(S) *Joseph Harker, E. H. Ryan and Alfred Terraine* (C) *Comelli and Lucile*	*Edward Royce*
TO-NIGHT'S THE NIGHT	105	Austen Hurgon	(S) *Joseph and Phil Harker* (C) *Comelli*	*George Shurley*
TONI	127	Herbert Bryan	(S) *Alfred Terraine and Phil Harker* (C) *Idare and Zimmerman*	*Jack Buchanan*
TOREADOR, THE	31, 32, 33		(S) *Joseph Harker and Hawes Craven* (C) *Wilhem*	*Willie Warde*
UNDER THE COUNTER	191	Jack Hulbert	(S) *Clifford Pember* (C) *Loraine, Hartnell, Kitty Foster, etc.*	*Jack Hulbert and John Gregory*
UNDER YOUR HAT	187	Jack Hulbert	(S) *Clifford Pember* (C) *Doris Zinkeisen*	*Jack Hulbert, Philip Buchel and John Byron*
VAGABOND KING, THE	147	Richard Boleslavsky	(S) & (C) *James Reynolds*	*Royal Cutter and Helen Grenelle*
VALMOUTH	211	Vida Hope	(S) & (C) *Tony Walton*	*Harry Naughton*
WALTZES FROM VIENNA	168	Hassard Short	(S) *Albert R. Johnson* (C) *Doris Zinkeisen*	*Albertina Rasch*

	(I)	(II)	(III)
WEST SIDE STORY 210	Jerome Robbins	(S) *Oliver Smith* (C) *Irene Sharaff*	*Jerome Robbins*
WHITE HORSE INN 166	Erik Charell	(S) & (C) *Ernst Stern*	*Max Rivers*
WHO'S HOOPER? 118	J. A. E. Malone	(S) *Conrad Tritschler and T. E. Ryan* (C) *Comelli*	*Willie Warde*
WONDER BAR 165	Julius B. Salter	(S) *Basil Ionides* (C) *Gordon Conway, La Rue, etc.*	*Fred Lord, Tilly Brisson and Hilda Beck*

SOURCES OF MUSICALS ILLUSTRATED (*Plays, Books, etc.*)

AUTHORS (including Lyricists) OF MUSICALS ILLUSTRATED

Rollit, George, 36
Ropes, Arthur Reed, see Ross, Adrian
Rose, L. Arthur, 183
Ross, Adrian, 2, 4, 10, 21, 27, 30, 31, 34, 38, 42, 47, 51, 64, 66, 69, 75, 77, 82, 84, 86, 89, 96, 98, 100, 106, 107, 112, 113, 122
Rubens, Paul, 28, 36, 39, 56, 57, 60, 71, 92, 96, 104, 105, 106, 112

Schanzer, Rudolph, 126, 170
Schwab, Laurence, 154
Shipp, Jesse A., 43
Simon, Neil, 226
Slade, Julian, 206
Smith, Paul Gerard, 157, 162
Sondheim, Stephen, 210
Spewack, Sam and Bella, 201

Starkie, Martin, 228
Stein, Joseph, 225
Stein, Leo, 66
Stewart, Michael, 222

Tanner, James T., 10, 30, 31, 38, 47, 51, 77, 86, 96, 98
Taylor, Charles H., 36, 40, 52, 55, 65
Taylor, Dwight, 173
Taylor, John, 224
Taylor, Ross, 224
Thompson, Alex M., 57, 79, 91, 93
Thompson, Frederick, 105, 111, 113, 118, 135, 142, 157, 163, 182, 184
Titheradge, Dion, 160
Travers, Ben, 128
Tudor, Anthony (Choreographer), 181

Turner, John Hastings, 130

Unger, Gladys, 100, 106

Wasserman, Dale, 229
Welisch, Ernest, 126, 170
Wells, William K., 135
Weston, R. P., 148, 149, 171, 179
Williams, Hugh and Margaret, 224
Willner, A. M., 82, 89, 122, 128, 168
Wilson, Sandy, 204, 211
Wimperis, Arthur, 57, 63, 79, 91, 92, 94, 143
Wodehouse, P. G., 63, 116, 117, 124, 144
Wright, Robert, 208
Wylie, Lauri, 143, 162

AUTHORS OF PLAYS, BOOKS, *etc.,* FROM WHICH MUSICALS ARE DRAWN

Aleichem, Sholem, 225
Arnold, Franz, 196

Bach, Ernest, 196
Besier, Rudolf, 221

Cervantes, Miguel de, 229
Chaucer, Geoffrey, 228

Davis, Richard Harding, 84
Dickens, Charles, 213, 219

Edgington, May, 138
Emerson, John, 185

Fellini, Federico, 226
Ferber, Edna, 153
Fielding, Henry, 212
Firbank, Ronald, 211
Flaiano, Ennio, 226

Glazer, Benjamin F., 199

Isham, Frederick S., 171
Isherwood, Christopher, 227

Knoblock, Edward, 208

Landon, Margaret, 203
Laver, James, 172
Locke, W. J., 72
Loos, Anita, 185, 217

Mandel, Frank, 138
McCarthy, Justin Huntley, 147
Melford, Austin, 196
Michener, James A., 200
Molnar, Ferenc, 199
Montgomery, James, 115, 171
Müller, Hans, 166

Nyitray, Emile, 138

Osborne, Hubert, 149

Pinelli, Tullio, 226
Pinero, Arthur, 113, 118

Riggs, Lynn, 194

Shaw, George Bernard, 209

Trapp, Maria Augusta, 214
Turner, John Hastings, 130

Van Druten, John, 227

Webster, Jean, 202
Wells, H. G., 218
White, T. H., 220
Wilder, Thornton, 222

Acknowledgements

Not only has the musical comedy stage received scant justice at the hands of the critics but it seems to have been assiduously neglected by any theatrical writers of serious reputation. The realms of light opera, often straying wrongly over the lines of demarcation, have been explored in *Origin and Development of Light Opera* by Sterling Mackinlay (Hutchinson 1928). The monumental *Complete Book of Light Opera* by Mark Lubbock (Putnam 1962) leans over backwards to record many works, which the authors and composers in their most sanguine moments would not have included! At the other end of the scale the books of W. Macqueen Pope are clothed with an Edwardian nostalgia and a romantic aura in which research and truth have little place. *The Rise of Opera in England* by Eric Walter White (John Lehmann 1951) tells excellently, with copious appendices, all one needs to know of the serious side of the roots of the English musical stage.

The only serious attempt to tell the story of musical comedy was made by Ernest Short in *Fifty Years of Vaudeville* (Eyre and Spottiswoode 1946). A misleading title under which the author tries to combine the realms of revue and music hall and that of the musical comedy stage. Unfortunately the book's inaccuracies stem from the fault which we may all fall into, unless great care is taken, when writing of a world we know personally, of being the fruits of reminiscence rather than of objective historical research.

American writers who have tried to treat the subject with respect have, through their own terms of reference, perforce been limited to their own country.

We have tried to put into story and picture the growth of the 'musical' over the past seventy-six years, and to choose representative pictures of stars, styles and situations which go to make up the traditions of musical comedy.

In our researches we have been helped by the Curator and staff of the Enthoven Collection of the Victoria and Albert Museum. Our especial thanks to Tony Lathem who read the book in its proof stages and gave invaluable advice for which we are deeply grateful.

We would also like to recognise the kindness of Raymond Howorth who was, as ever, ready to help in many ways. We are also indebted to W. A. Darlington and *The Daily Telegraph* for allowing us to quote from his valedictory article.

We would like to thank the following press representatives for their unfailing courtesy and help, Vivienne Byerley, Roger Clifford, Theo Cowan, Torrington Douglas and Jack Ingham. Also the offices of the following managements, Donald Albery, Peter Bridge, Harold Fielding, Emile Littler, Richard Pilbrow, The Theatre Royal, Bristol, The Mermaid Theatre and The Players' Theatre.

The following photographers' work is reproduced: Cecil Beaton, 209, Michael Boys,

204, 205, 212, Tom Hustler, 214, 215, 217, 218, 220, 224, 226, Angus McBean, 188, 194, 197, 198, 200, 203, 210, 221, 222, Alec Murray, 213, Morris Newcombe, 230, David Redfern, 219, Houston Rogers, 201, 202, 208, David Sim, 211, Roger Wood, 207.

We have once again to thank Frances Fleetwood for compiling the index, Mary Quinnell for her patient mastering of our manuscript and making it into a readable typescript and Vera Seaton-Reid for her usual material assistance.

Last but by no means least our grateful thanks to Noël Coward for his foreword.

'If the Theatre were to be shut up, the Stage wholly silenced
and suppressed, I believe the world, bad as it is now, would be
ten times more wicked.'

ANTOINE HOUDARD DE LA MOTTE

(*Playwright and librettist* 1672–1731)

[64]